HABOO

Native American Stories
from Puget Sound

SECOND EDITION

TRANSLATED AND EDITED BY
VI HILBERT

FOREWORD BY
JILL La POINTE

INTRODUCTION BY
THOM HESS

ILLUSTRATIONS BY
RON HILBERT/COY

UNIVERSITY OF WASHINGTON PRESS
Seattle

www.tulalipcares.org

Haboo was supported by a generous grant from the Tulalip Tribes Charitable Fund, which provides the opportunity for a sustainable and healthy community for all.

Composed in Noto, typeface designed by Google

24 23 22   5 4

Printed and bound in the United States of America

UNIVERSITY OF WASHINGTON PRESS
uwapress.uw.edu

LIBRARY OF CONGRESS CATALOGING-IN-PUBLICATION DATA ON FILE
LC record available at https://lccn.loc.gov/2019041051
LC ebook record available at https://lccn.loc.gov/2019041052

ISBN 978-0-295-74697-5 (hardcover), ISBN 978-0-295-74696-8 (paperback),
ISBN 978-0-295-74698-2 (ebook)

Map by Laura Dassow

Vi Hilbert, wearing a dress of pounded cedar, 1984

*Vi Hilbert taught courses in Lushootseed language and literature
in the American Indian Studies Program at the University of Washington
and to various tribal groups. She was well known as a gifted storyteller
and interpreter of her oral traditions.*

CONTENTS

FOREWORD TO THE SECOND EDITION

When *Haboo* was first published thirty-five years ago, the dramatic art of traditional storytelling in many of our Native American communities was fading as younger generations became more adapted to mainstream culture and values. Recognizing the impact of cultural change taking place in their communities, my grandmother—like so many other elders—sought to gather and preserve as much traditional information and wisdom as possible. Every elder who contributed to this magnificent collection of cultural stories did so in hopes that someday future generations will once again appreciate the ancient art of storytelling.

Although much has changed over the years, there remains one unfortunate constant. Despite all the technological advancements since the first publication of *Haboo*, our communities continue to lose many of their beloved elders. As each year passes, we are left with fewer and fewer among us who can still recite the ancient stories and even fewer who can retell the stories in our traditional Lushootseed language. Confronting this reality remains as critical to the survival of Coast Salish culture and language today as it was thirty-five years ago. The wisdom and teachings found in *Haboo* continue to offer a pedagogical resource that highlights a way of being in the world that we have strayed from, and they remain as relevant today as they have been for generations.

Growing up, my brother Jay and I heard our grandmother Vi taqʷšəblu Hilbert tell many of the stories included here over and over again. Staying true to who she was, she never explained the meaning or revealed the overall lessons hidden in the stories, but rather she instructed us to think about each story and ask ourselves, "What is the story trying to tell me?" It wasn't until years later that I gained a deep appreciation for the traditional art of storytelling, as I heard Grandma repeat to audiences everywhere, young and old, that "Lushootseed never insults the intelligence of a listener by explaining the story," allowing them the same dignity her elders allowed her, to find their own interpretation and understanding. Over the years I have personally found this to be true insofar as my own encounters with the stories have remained fluid, growing with me, teaching me something new about myself as life brings me new experiences. I have been perplexed by some stories for years, only to realize that the lessons within are unveiled over time, bit by bit in accordance with my own physical and spiritual location in life at any given time.

The Lushootseed language and culture arose from the oral traditions of the Puget Sound Coast Salish people. It wasn't until the late 1960s and early 1970s that Lushootseed was developed into its current written form. It is important to appreciate this, given how easily technological advances allow us to access information. Today, finding the answer to nearly any question or learning about something new is as simple as asking Google, Alexa, or Siri. Since the advent of the internet and the rapid development of smartphones, nearly limitless information is available at our fingertips. Nearly all tribal communities throughout Puget Sound have language revitalization programs that use dedicated websites, YouTube, and smartphone apps to promote their cultural languages. Any person with a computer or smartphone can start learning Lushootseed. I have no doubt that my grandmother would be not only amazed but excited about how technology has furthered preservation and promotion of the Lushootseed language and culture. However, it is also important to acknowledge how technology has changed the way we process information into knowledge that can enhance the quality of our lives.

Long before Lushootseed was developed into a written language, the ability to listen carefully and remember what you heard was intrinsic to the longevity and continuity of all important Coast Salish cultural teachings. Everything from family lineages and cultural traditions to spiritual and religious praxis, as well as our creation stories, which provide us an ontological understanding of our place and role in creation, were entrusted to the minds and memories of the listener, especially those who excelled in developing their minds, such as my grandmother's Aunt Susie Sampson Peter. For countless generations, the safeguarding of all this information depended not only on our ability to develop extraordinary memories but more importantly on our ability to listen attentively: "ləshuyud dču? kʷ(i) adx̌əč." Make yourself single-minded (to avoid confusion). Moreover, development of these skills and abilities extended far beyond the preservation and transfer of information—they played a crucial role in our ontological purview. Understanding our place and role in creation was shaped through our ability to listen and learn from creation in all its forms. My grandmother often repeated a common phrase she learned from her elders: "dᶻixʷ dxʷ?ugʷusał ti?ə? swatixʷtəd." The earth is our first teacher.

For countless generations our ancestors sought guidance from Mother Nature by listening carefully to all the teachings she had to offer, revealing to each person their vocation as well as moral guidance in how we are to conduct ourselves in the world. As each generation passes, our ability to listen carefully and remember accurately have faded. The skills of old continue to wane ever further as technology relieves us of the historical necessity to memorize important information. Today, children are no longer required to sit patiently for hours listening to the old ones tell and retell us our cultural stories. No longer are children required to listen as the elders teach us our family histories and lineages or instill our spiritual and religious practices. All these vitally important teachings are x̌əčusədə? and xʷdikʷ, the special information that guides us throughout our lives.

What impact does the loss of such a rich and meaningful component of life have on the people or society? We are fortunate that our ancestors had the wisdom to foresee the tremendous change coming that would inexorably dismantle the world they once knew so well. Although it broke their hearts to know that these changes would affect every aspect of Puget Sound Coast Salish culture and life, they remained willing and determined to seize any opportunity to share their wisdom through what Swinomish elder Susie Sampson Peter called "a different canoe" (the tape recorder), so it could be captured and made available to us. We are also blessed by the foresight of scholars such as Pamela Amoss, Sally Snyder, Thom Hess, and retired educator Leon Metcalf, whose fascination with the people and compassion for a dying culture led them to devote hundreds of hours traveling around the region, visiting different elders, and recording their wisdom, histories, and stories.

The stories in *Haboo* have so much to offer. They give each of us an opportunity to escape the seemingly unending technological bombardment of information and useless distractions streamed at us high-speed through our smartphones, laptops, iPads, and televisions twenty-four hours a day. I encourage you to take a break, shut down your laptop or iPad, turn off the TV, put your phone on silent, and allow yourself some time to sit quietly with at least one of the stories included here. Give yourself time to think about what unique meaning or lesson a story has for you. And if you feel ambitious, memorize it and share it with others.

ʔutigʷicid čəd (I THANK YOU)

Jill tsisqʷux̌ʷał La Pointe

Jill tsisqʷux̌ʷał La Pointe is granddaughter of Vi taqʷšəblu Hilbert and holds a master's of social work from the University of Washington. She is director of Lushootseed Research, a nonprofit organization dedicated to sustaining Lushootseed language and culture and to enhancing cross-cultural knowledge, wisdom, and relations.

NOTE ON ORTHOGRAPHY

With the permission and oversight of the Vi taqʷšəblu Hilbert family, this second edition of *Haboo* has been updated so that x-wedge characters (x̌) are used in place of x-dots. Lushootseed is an active, living language, and the orthography has evolved since the first edition of *Haboo* was published in 1985. The documentation of the language continues to be refined, and this second edition has been updated to reflect current orthography.

FOREWORD TO THE FIRST EDITION

This collection of traditional stories is the selection and translation of a remarkable woman, Mrs. Vi taqʷšəblu Hilbert, a Skagit Indian of the Northern Lushootseed of Western Washington. She grew up among her people in the Skagit valley at a time when Native people throughout the Northwest had already been forced to adjust to the white economy and kinds of work. It was, nevertheless, a period when many of the old social patterns survived; and most importantly, it was a time when everyone still spoke the ancestral language fluently. In fact, many elders of that day did not know English.

Therefore, as a little girl taqʷšəblu learned Lushootseed as her first language and, along with it, the values and beliefs of her people. She saw the old longhouse traditions. She also began to acquire a knowledge of the land and the Native way of relating to it.

However, the white world eventually intruded. She attended a number of schools in northern Washington as her father moved from place to place seeking work during the Great Depression. At several of these, she suffered the meanness of white classmates, who reflected their parents' prejudice against Washington's first people. But taqʷšəblu persevered. Instead of leaving school as many other Native children have done in similar circumstances, she chose to attend Chemawa, an Indian boarding school in Oregon. This decision was a wise one; but it did take her away from her own people and began to weaken her contacts with Lushootseed language and culture.

Although life at Chemawa was pleasant, she realized that she was not getting the best education possible; therefore, with characteristic determination, and some anxiety, she enrolled in Franklin High School in Portland.

She supported herself by working seven days a week as a housekeeper. Residing in this home required her to walk 36 blocks to school. She did well at Franklin and received high praise from the principal upon graduation.

After being graduated, she married and had several children. She helped support her family through outside work. Among other occupations, she ran a restaurant, owned a hairdressing business, trained as a telegrapher, and was secretary to the Director of Nursing at Children's Orthopedic Hospital in Seattle. She did not, however, return to the Skagit valley to live. Her memory of Lushootseed continued to fade.

Nevertheless, she felt the need for her ancestral heritage all through her busy young adult life. After the death of her parents, she began to tape record songs and stories from her relatives. Fluency in Lushootseed and the way of life it represented gradually returned to her. In 1967 she heard from some of her people about a linguist named Hess, who was writing a grammar and dictionary of her language. She decided to meet this scholar, who had a system for writing the sounds of Lushootseed, which had not had an alphabet before. With some initial trepidation, she began to learn to read and write the language of her childhood and very quickly mastered both. She then threw herself headlong into the task of recording and translating as much Lushootseed oral tradition as possible.

Shortly after beginning this new endeavor, however, she suffered a severe stroke which halted all language work for a long, long time. Through this dark period the need she felt to preserve the ways of her people never abated. Eventually, this conviction plus immense determination prevailed over an illness that would have stopped most people. She learned to read and write the language all over again, and began collaborating with the linguist on a number of articles and a two-volume pedagogical grammar of Lushootseed. In 1972 she began teaching the language at the University of Washington and in 1976 added a course on the literature in English translation.

taqʷšəblu has now given up most other activities, devoting herself almost exclusively to analyzing, teaching, and archiving her language and culture. It is no ordinary eight-hour day that she gives to this task. From well before sunrise until very late at night, she works day in and day out, interrupted only by trips to various reservations to meet her responsibilities as an elder and to interview older friends and relatives who have special knowledge about the old ways. A vast wealth of information is now available solely because of her unflagging efforts. Many are deeply indebted to her outstanding achievements: the scholarly community—linguists, anthropologists, and folklorists—as well as the coming generations of Lushootseed people and all others interested in Native languages and traditions.

THOMAS HESS
Department of Linguistics
University of Victoria

PREFACE

sʔabałx̌əč (SHARED THOUGHTS)

Haboo is my third volume of texts from the oral traditions of the Lushootseed Salish of Western Washington. The first, *Yəhaẃ*, and the second, *Huboo*, were privately published for use by my students in a Lushootseed literature class at the University of Washington. I have managed to transcribe many more stories since then, which makes the publication of this third volume possible. In a future volume I hope to bring to the public another collection of tales in the original Lushootseed with accompanying English translations.

We do not know how long it has taken for these stories to come down to us, for we did not use the kind of calendar everyone uses today. My people marked time by referring to especially remarkable occasions, such as the year of the solar eclipse, or the period when the big log jam still blocked the Skagit river, or when the longhouses at slux̌ (Lyman-Hamilton) still stood, or the time before the King George (British) people came. All of our culture had to be committed to memory. To this end, our historians developed excellent memories in order to pass on important information to later generations.

Our legends are like gems with many facets. They need to be read, savored, and reread from many angles. My elders never said to me, "This story carries such and such a meaning." I was expected to listen carefully and learn why the story was being told. Though guided, I was allowed the dignity of finding my own interpretation.

To my sorrow, the art of storytelling among my people is nearly forgotten. Television and books have supplanted the role of the Lushootseed raconteurs. Hopefully, this collection will preserve something of their knowledge and verbal artistry. In the old days, stories were told at home. Some elders have told me that homes without good storytellers would invite skilled narrators to visit.

Most of those who have contributed stories to this volume were relatives or people I knew or often visited with my parents when I was a child. It has been a great pleasure to listen to their voices on recorded tape and to be able to transcribe the language phonetically before translating into English. Their voices tell me when to anticipate anger, humor, joy, sarcasm, distances in time or space, tenderness, compassion, and love. We have no word for love in Lushootseed, so it is good to be able to recognize its signals. It is also important for you to know that everything is possible in Lushootseed culture, because we have no word for *can't*. We also have no words that say, *hello, good morning, good night, or thank you*. We can express thanks by saying ʔudahadubš čəxʷ—You have done me a great favor / I appreciate what you have done for me; and by ʔuṫigʷicid čəd (ṫigʷ comes from the word ṫiwiɫ, to pray)—I offer prayerful thanks to you. Most often, we express thanks by raising both arms and slightly moving the open palms up and down. This is a gesture of thankfulness and respect.

When the culture was solely oral, as some elders would prefer to have it remain, the legends and other information were recited often in order to keep it alive and point up moral lessons.

All of the stories give expression to the most important values of our culture. So that they can be better appreciated, I list them here. Ordinarily, they are learned so as to become second nature. Our elders made frequent reference to these values, but like everything else, people had to figure all of them out for themselves. These are the ones I heard most often as a child and still hear at public gatherings of our people. Many of the values are phrased in the negative, but I have expressed them here in the positive as do English speakers.

Respect (Hold Sacred) All of the Earth—
  ʔəsḱʷiʔa(t)txʷ tiʔəʔ bəəəkʷ swatixʷtəd
Respect (Hold Sacred) All of the Spirits—
  ʔəsḱʷiʔa(t)txʷ kʷi tuiʔal sqəlalitut

Remember (Hold Sacred) The Creator—

ʔəsk̓ʷiʔa(t)txʷ kʷi x̌ax̌aʔ šəq siʔab

Be Honest—x̌ʷi kʷ(i)adsubədčəb (Don't You Dare Lie!)

Be Generous—ləskʷaxʷad kʷ(i)adʔiišəd

(Be Helpful to Your People in Any Way You Can!)

Be Compassionate—ʔəsʔušəbid kʷ(i)adʔiišəd

(Feel Forgiveness for Others!)

Be Clean—ʔəsċaʔkʷ čəxʷ (You Will Be Washed)

ʔəsċaʔkʷ tul̓ʔal bək̓ʷ saʔ (sċiq̓ʷil ʔi dᶻək̓ʷadad)

(Keep Washing Away All Badness (Dirt and Sin–Crime))

Be Industrious—čəxʷaʔ ck̓ʷaqid łuləyayus

(And You Will Work Always, Don't Be Lazy!)

As you read the stories you will learn that Coyote, Mink, and Raven provide us with negative examples because their behaviors are usually contrary to our teachings. Children would *never* be like these characters when properly instructed. All of us were told, again and again, you are *not* to disgrace yourself or your people under any circumstances. Still, people appreciate anyone smart enough to get something done by fooling someone else. We all enjoy the humor of human foibles and frailties, but because they are done here by people with animal names, we can laugh more openly about them.

Otherwise, Native people are very careful in public. No one should be made to feel embarrassed or unwanted. We genuinely appreciate differences. Although the characters get themselves in lots of trouble, they are not wiped out at the end. All life is respected. Wisely, they are allowed to stew in their own folly, and figure their own way out of the situation.

Among my people, disapproval is shown by silently ignoring someone, but even this is only temporary. Everyone should be made to feel welcome and, therefore, important. Bad habits are overlooked. Unwise activity might lead to ridicule, but this was a way to help the person overcome the difficulty.

The stories also include references to earthy substances. Seeing them in this collection might make the reader think that people talked this way all the time. This was not so. Relations between men and women were very modest. Functions like passing gas, urinating, and mating were male subjects, like locker room humor. They form the basis of profanity, just as they do in English. Still, anatomy was never mentioned in public. It was too gross. A properly raised girl or woman used only dainty vocabulary, although older women might joke among themselves.

All of the stories are rich in humor, but outsiders might find it hard to recognize. Much of it pokes fun at pretensions. Some is sarcastic. In speech, this is done with voice inflection and rhetorical questions *He's so smart, isn't he?* The tone indicates that the statement is contrary to fact. Such subtleties are keenly appreciated, bringing people down to size and reminding everyone of the comforts of belonging together. My people can laugh at themselves and others in a way that is not malicious. It is mutually enjoyable and frequently uplifting.

Now let me tell you a bit about the storytellers you are about to meet. (Detailed information on the texts themselves is given in Appendix 2.)

My parents, CHARLEY and LOUISE ANDERSON, told stories and historical information to each other all the time, just to remind and refresh themselves. They also sang our ancestral songs to remember them, often when we were driving or alone in the mountains. They told me stories at home whenever I coaxed one or both of them. I understand that among some groups, storytelling took place only in the winter time. They were told to me anytime, but then I was away at school all winter. My parents had different styles. My father was laconic, soft-spoken, and detailed. My mother was dramatic, making much of the personalities and situations.

Although I knew all of the storytellers in my Haboo books, I did not hear some of their stories until 1967 when I began working with the tapes made by Leon Metcalf. In the 1950s, at his own expense, he visited many of our knowledgeable elders and recorded stories, messages, songs, and history.

I remember that when we visited EMMA CONRAD, we had to park our car near the river, honk the horn and wait for Emma to get in her shovelnose canoe and bring us across. We would stay for a day or so. She did not tell stories when we visited because everyone was too busy catching up on the news. I played outdoors with her daughter and son. In later years she lived alone. She was gentle and soft-spoken. Most people knew that the epic "Story of the Seasons" (The All Year Round Story) was recited by the Conrads and the Enicks. Emma was born an Enick and married a Conrad.

ANNIE DANIELS is someone I met on the tapes. She and my Aunt Susie Peter sent messages back and forth. Her Fly story gave me lots of exercise transcribing Southern Lushootseed, but the content was so fascinating that I am still trying to unravel it. I have more bridges to cross before I will be satisfied. Along the way, several fine speakers have helped me. They learned the southern dialect as children, but as adults, they have moved all over Puget Sound. Fortunately, the knowledge they learned and their language has stayed with them.

I met AGNES JAMES on the tapes, too, singing songs and telling stories. Later, at Tulalip, I saw cattail dolls that she had made, so she also must have been a weaver. Her style is informal and borrows Giants from nursery tales.

I remember the big, booming voice of ANDREW (SPAN) JOE. He was an active and important member of the Swinomish community and the Longhouse religion. His ancestors were Skagit and Canadian. I heard him speak and sing on many occasions, and he was always impressive. I never heard him tell stories, probably because he was not a relative.

HARRY MOSES and his wife Jessie were relatives and fellow members of the Shaker church. They lived mainly in the Upper Skagit area, relocating as often as we did. We visited quite often because they and my parents thoroughly enjoyed each other's company. As they exchanged reminiscences, I loved to listen in. Harry had a wonderful sense of humor, which was well known. He loved to tell stories and his audience knew that they could count on him to embellish the facts, with a twinkle in his eyes. *Why, Harry saw the eyes of the woman in the moon, and the fish he caught in the Cascade river behind his house were so big that when he lifted them onto his shoulder, the tails would drag far behind him on the ground.*

My cousin RAY PAUL, born in 1910, lives at Swinomish and has long shared his stories with LaConner school children and community elders. He enjoys creating songs in Lushootseed out of his stories and other events. One of my favorites translates as "my washtub has no barnacles." He speaks effectively in public and urges everyone to uphold our traditions. Although he is now blind, he still lives alone and takes care of himself. Sometimes, he does his own canning.

My aunt, SUSIE SAMPSON PETER, was a highly respected historian, who carried a heavy responsibility to pass on our culture. She and my dad were from the same family and their interest in perpetuating cultural information had been instilled by the wise teachings of their ancestors. We visited her and her husband, William Peter, often. I always stayed to listen as they ate, visited, and attended Shaker and Longhouse services. I would be put to bed on or under a bench, while the noise of the rituals reverberated around me. She sometimes joined us working in the berry fields to earn some money. Every day, I would remove blackberry thorns from her hands. Her eyes were so weak, she picked by feel. She was so special that even my students all call her Aunt Susie.

She was a highly sophisticated raconteuse. She respected the traditional form of our stories, using the ancient beginning: *Somebody lived there.* She always recounted the events four times before the story came to a close. She would keep count for the audience, reminding everyone how many times this or that had happened so far in the story. She always ended in the traditional way, either diɫ(s)šaċs or diɫ shuys—both mean "that's the end."

She gave a performance when she told a tale. She became the character in the story, using stylized speech for some characters. Raven always speaks with a nasal twang. She created spirit power songs for Bear, Deer, and Flounder in the story of Mink's House Party. She had interpretations for the personalities of all of her characters. She even gave voice to a dead log that was brought to life to be a babysitter for Star Child.

Aunt Susie did not speak English. Her son Alfonso was usually present to interpret for Leon Metcalf. He asked her to begin a story by saying "habuəxʷ k̓ʷuyəʔ—*Go ahead now Mother, tell a story.*" When she was into the story, she reminded everyone to say "habu" every so often. For the benefit of English speakers, I have also spelled it as "haboo." This is the customary response from the audience to assure the storyteller that they were awake and attentive. Al also said "habu" to prompt his mother if she was hesitating over some section of the story that was eluding her memory.

Her oldest son, MARTIN SAMPSON, told me that the dialect she spoke was the oldest of our Skagit languages. Her vocabulary was mostly the same as that of my parents, but she included words in the legends that were not used every day. Martin helped me translate her stories because he spoke her dialect and had the same desire to pass on our culture. His book, *Indians of Skagit County*, is treasured by us for its documentation of tribal areas, as well as the sketch of our history. When I asked Martin to define

Native culture for my students and me, he said that it was "learning from the land."

After Aunt Susie became totally blind, she lived with Martin in Tacoma. Her daughter-in-law, Cecelia (Betty) told me this poignant story. Susie's bedroom was next to the kitchen and every day Cecelia could hear her telling legends to herself, while sitting alone. One day, she began a story but stopped after a few sentences, saying "Oh no, I told that one yesterday."

To the end of her days, she practiced the teachings of our culture. In order to fulfill the responsibilities of a cultural historian, she repeated her vital information every day so it would not be forgotten.

ALICE WILLIAMS lives on the new Upper Skagit reservation near Sedro-Woolley. She learned her stories from an old woman from east of the Cascades, probably Nespelem on the Colville Reservation. Her large family is very proud of her knowledge of their cultural heritage. She is one of the few people among the Skagit who can still make baskets in the old way with cedar bark and cedar roots. Recently, I asked her if she remembered how to make traditional cedar bark clothing. She said she did, and made a dress for me to buy.

LUCY WILLIAMS, one of the favorite storytellers of Dr. Sally Snyder, was quiet, soft-spoken, and helpful. She was married to Dick Williams, my uncle. We sometimes visited them in Concrete when they lived near the Shaker church. She was often one of the cooks for Shaker meetings. Her bawdy stories came as a surprise to me, but Skunk has become a favorite with all readers because it is so different and outrageous. It makes fine use of this character. She spoke Skagit well and was good natured, but stayed mostly in the background in deference to her husband.

My cousin WALT WILLIAMS lives with his wife in Nooksack territory. He said he had forgotten all of the stories he heard as a boy, but I coaxed him into telling the four short ones presented here. He is fluent in our language and a willing consultant. Long ago, he built a longhouse which is used every winter for the rituals of our ancestral religion.

Some readers might be interested to know that this collection represents several generations. Alice Williams is the daughter of Lucy; Martin is the son of Aunt Susie, and Ron Hilbert/Coy is the grandson of Louise and Charley Anderson.

In addition to these storytellers, there are others I would like to honor. Public storytelling is no longer customary, but these people have been active in teaching about the importance of stories and the rest of our traditions. Some of them discuss the "meaning" of stories and give them morals.

My cousin Isadore (pətius) Tom, spiritual leader who lives on the Lummi Reservation, has told stories for many years in the public schools of his area. Some of his stories were included in the first volume of Huboo.

My cousin Harriet Shelton Dover has long done the same in the Tulalip and Marysville area. Her story of Mud Swallow appears in the first Huboo and I told it at the dedication of the Upper Skagit community building.

Fillmore James is another Tulalip elder, who has shared his knowledge in the public schools of Marysville. He also is fond of Country and Western music, as students in my university classes have heard. He reminds us that our people can appreciate many different traditions.

Gary Hillaire, a Lummi carver and nephew of Isadore Tom, speaks in schools about the legends he has illustrated.

I have encouraged my son Ron (čadesqidəb) Hilbert/Coy to become the storyteller for my family, as well as my illustrator. I thank thank him for all his efforts. I thank my daughter for her gentle encouragement over the years. Sometimes, when my schedule allows, I do tell stories in public, but I prefer to be a translator rather than a narrator.

One of my students, Rebecca Chamberlain Fenwick, is keenly interested in our Lushootseed literature and culture. She is doing her master's thesis on the stories and is very sensitive to their meaning. I have encouraged her to memorize and tell stories to interested groups.

Long ago, there were stories which were claimed by individual families; others were forbidden to tell them. At present, I am not aware of any restrictions, except that the original storyteller retains a native copyright.

I advise all of my students that I have published our literature because I want the world to know and appreciate this central part of our culture. It conveys much of our ancient richness and complexities. I also encourage interested students of our literature to memorize and retell the stories *as* I have translated them, so they will be faithful to the original Lushootseed. Further, they are to familiarize themselves with as much of the cultural background as possible. The storyteller and his or her community are always to be acknowledged and given credit.

I am grateful to all of our people who allowed their voices to be recorded and appreciate the scholars who realized the value of using a tape recorder after they became available. Leon Metcalf, who now lives in Arizona, will always be honored for his generous efforts and for donating the tapes to the University of Washington.

Dr. Thomas Melville Hess, a linguist now at the University of Victoria, British Columbia, has earned an important place in our hearts and minds. He has given us the results of many years of careful research and professional skill, begun with his dissertation at the University of Washington. He shuns praise; but the Lushootseed believe that well deserved praise must be voiced. I will always thank him for believing in my ability when I was uncertain that I could ever learn to read, write, and transcribe Lushootseed. I have always had copies of all of his work.

Dr. Pamela Amoss of Bellevue has always helped and encouraged my endeavors. She knew my parents and has become part of my family. Both Drs. Hess and Amoss were students of Dr. Melville Jacobs of the Anthropology Department at the University of Washington. Dr. Jacobs encouraged his students to study the language and culture of the first inhabitants of this region. All of us have benefitted from their careful research.

Dr. Sally Snyder, another of these students, worked among my people collecting folklore, which she wrote down only in English. She has graciously given me permission to include some of these stories here, as well as in the first volume. Carl Cary, a Bellingham poet, gave me copies of his fieldwork among the Upper Skagit people. Virginia Mohling recorded songs from my dad and Dr. Jacobs made them available to me. We are grateful for all these contributions and, also, for the materials on Suquamish assembled by Dr. Warren Snyder now at Sacramento State College.

To date, my primary research grants have been from the Elizabeth and Melville Jacobs Fund. I thank my husband, Henry Donald Hilbert, for providing support for Lushootseed Research, a non-profit organization, newly incorporated with the help of Jack Fiander. Any royalties from the sale of *Haboo* will be contributed toward its goals.

Many of my students and friends are providing invaluable help bringing the research up to date with current technology. Lushootseed has joined the computer age. It is being fed into a new being, the generous gift of a former student. Eventually, after many laborious hours by Pam (wiw̓su)

Cahn, Dr. Toby Langen, Dr. Jay Miller, and Crisca Bierwert Russell, Lushootseed will fully benefit from the magical skills of computers. My farsighted elders would be delighted to know that their centuries-old memories will have a new life thanks to another kind of memory storage. Now it can benefit young people in additional ways. Youth, the source for future generations and the well being of all humanity, can continue to be enriched by the xʷdikʷ—the wisdom, teachings, philosophy, and advice—distilled by the dxʷləšucid the primal Lushootseed.

Incentive for developing Lushootseed teaching materials was provided by the classes in the American Indian Studies Program at the University of Washington that Dr. Hess and I began teaching in 1972. Lushootseed raises its hands to say "thank you" for the chance to share our knowledge.

In much of the text, {anything set off by brackets} is my commentary, unless otherwise specified.

And so, finally, I am done.

(dᶻaakʼʷuʔəxʷ čəd huy.)

VI (taqʷšəblu) HILBERT
Seattle, Washington
October 1984

INTRODUCTION

THOMAS HESS

This volume presents to the English reading public translations of 33 traditional stories of the Lushootseed-speaking peoples of western Washington State. Lushootseed is one of some twenty Native languages comprising the Salish family, spoken over much of Washington, British Columbia, and parts of Idaho, Montana, and Oregon. Lushootseed itself is the name of the Native language of the Puget Sound region.

Along each of the rivers that flows into the Sound and on the many islands, small differences of accent, grammar, and vocabulary have arisen during the many centuries that Native people have dwelled there. Particularly noticeable are the differences separating the speakers of Lushootseed in the territories to the north of the present Snohomish-King County line from those living south of it. The cultures of the people to the north and south also differ in certain small ways. In their literature, the most obvious difference is the pattern or ritual number. In the north it is four, while in the south it is five.

All but one of the stories in this collection are from the Northern Lushootseed. The exception is *Fly* told by Annie Daniels, a speaker of Southern Lushootseed.

Many Lushootseed speaking people divide their oral literature into two categories, history called ləlaʔuləb and Myth Age stories known as sx̌ʷiʔab in the south and as syəyəhub/sx̌ʷiʔab (or simply syəhub) in the north. In addition to these two genres, there are also personal accounts which fall under the general term syəcəb which refers to any sort of news or non-traditional story. All the tales in this collection are syəyəhub/sx̌ʷiʔab.

Most syəyəhub are fairly light and humorous, reflecting the foibles of human nature. Although their themes are treated lightly, almost every story serves to teach appropriate behavior. This instruction is usually achieved by humorously detailing the unfortunate, even disastrous, consequences of breaking taboos.

A few of the traditional stories, however, have a more serious tone. Typically, these are longer than the lighter ones, and they are concerned with graver questions. They examine the world order and deal with points of tension within the social fabric. Their major characters are heroes who act wisely rather than impetuously or foolishly as in the lighter stories.

However, this dichotomy into lighter, shorter tales and longer, graver ones is only a tendency. Elements characteristic of one type of syəyəhub are frequently heard in the other; the Lushootseed people themselves do not judge the difference sufficient to warrant separate Lushootseed terms for the two types.

The events recounted in syəyəhub took place before the world was transformed. Long ago, before the change, there were no humans as we know them. All of the beings of this age shimmered among humanoid, animal, and spirit forms; but they always had the same emotions and sensibilities as humans. When people did arrive, the world had been prepared for them by the transformer, who had arranged for all of the beings to take on the fixed forms of animals, plants, and geological features. During the Myth Age, beings had some of the characteristics of the modern species with the same names. In addition, some of the denizens of the old world order have some of the characteristics we know them for today. For example, Raven, when a man, could fly and he was an unbridled glutton, an apt parallel to the scavenging habits of the present birds.

These characters, each with human and animal traits, provide the raconteur with great flexibility. He can draw upon one or the other of these attributes as plot, imagination, and sense of humor require. Consider the brief story about the sisters Boil and Hammer. They looked and acted just like people, except they ate only berries. At the same time, however, they were like a real boil and a real stone maul. Therefore, Boil burst when a fir needle fell on her head and Hammer drowned when she fell into the river because, after all, she was stone. In the old stories, the raconteur can have it both ways.

Supernatural power, a potency neutral in and of itself, is a third attribute of the early beings who preceded humans on the earth. By means of this power, they performed feats that no creature, human or otherwise, could do today. Frequently they had an amazing extra sense that told them who was responsible for some act when they themselves had not been present. Often, these powers resemble the magic of Western tradition but sometimes they are like the Lushootseed notion of spirit power (see Amoss 1978 and Jilek 1974).

The old order did not last however. At some time in the remote past a being of great power walked through the world changing everything into its present form, preparing the land for the Native people who were soon to come. Such a transformation is succinctly described at the end of *Mink and the Changer.*

Before this great transformation, there existed several worlds besides the one that people came to inhabit. Additionally, there was the sky world, the far away land of the Salmon People, and others. These other worlds were more or less similar to each other and it was possible to travel from one to another. Thus, other dimensions of existence were more than just theoretical constructs for the Lushootseed, as is particularly apparent in *Fly* and *Journey to the Sky and Back Down to Earth.*

Three beings of the prechange era are particularly prominent in Lushootseed literature. These are Mink, Raven, and Coyote. All three are trickster, impulsive characters who are utterly incapable of controlling their appetites and passions. No deception is too immoral or dishonest for them when trying to gratify their base desires. Their attempts at deception are often farfetched and always humorous. As often as they trick others, they themselves are either tricked or caught in their duplicity. And yet these amoral fellows do, on occasion, rise to heroic deeds for the benefit of others. For example, it was Mink and Raven who managed to procure daylight for their people.

One might wonder why Lushootseed is endowed with three tricksters. First, only Mink and Raven are indigenous. Coyote appears in stories from east of the Cascade Mountains, where coyotes are native. Puget Sound and the rest of western Washington were outside of their territory, although a few have wandered into the region quite recently. People of the coast some-times married people of the interior, so it likely that Coyote stories were taken into Lushootseed along with in-laws from the sagebrush country. Secondly, although Mink and Raven are both tricksters and totally unprin-cipled, they represent different facets of the human psyche. Raven is the glutton, Mink is the rake. The exploits of all three are a delight to hear described by the old storytellers.

While the characters in syəyəhub belong to the prehuman era, their inter–relationships reflect the social organization of Lushootseed speaking peoples before contact with Europeans. In precontact society, there were high class people, who in most villages probably constituted the majority, a small number of low class people, and slaves at the bottom. High class status was based on wealth and proper conduct. The wealth was measured in goods produced and natural resources controlled, along with what West-erners would consider to be intangibles. These included rights to songs, dances, and other features of important ceremonies. From the high class came the most influential men who, by virtue of their rank and prestige, oversaw the activities of the village. Political influence rarely extended beyond the local community.

The low class had little of either the material or intangible wealth and, worse, did not always conduct themselves appropriately. They lacked good manners. The most stigmatized of all, of course, were the slaves, who were taken in raids, traded from owners, or born of slave parents.

This social structure was not rigid. Someone from the lower class could, through skill and diligence, achieve higher status by gaining wealth and knowledge, most especially some of the all important advice called xʷdikʷ. The achievements of successful people also required spiritual powers, which they actively sought during personal quests in remote areas. High class families often had special places for acquiring such powers, which were used by succeeding generations. Conversely, a person born into high status could lose rank if lazy or incompetent.

Older siblings inherited more than their younger brothers and sisters, and this may have led to sibling rivalry on occasion. The traditional stories seem to side with the underdog, the youngest and, therefore, the most dis-advantaged sibling. It is always the youngest who is the wisest, most clever, and most successful when the older ones fail. The special abilities of the youngest sibling are well illustrated in *Wolf Brothers Kill Elk and Beaver*. Even the highly acculturated *Legend of the Three Sisters* notes that the youngest sister is the most beautiful.

Translating the literature of one language into another is never easy, especially when the cultures involved are extremely dissimilar. The task is made even more difficult when the translator must also render in writing what has been an oral tradition. In this collection of translations, taqʷšəblu has elected to flesh out the terse style of the original tales, with additions appropriate to English prose and essential for the Western reader's understanding.

The reader can gather some notion of the differences between Lushootseed and English by contrasting the following literal translation of the beginning of *Mink and the Changer* (p. 54) with the first paragraph of the published story.

(1) There was Mink. (2) Mink, it was, walking about.
(3) Yes, Mink was walking about. (4) Mink was walking.
(5) And then he came upon him:

(6) Mink, as is his way, steals the old fellow's roasting salmon.
(7) He steals the salmon roasting on the old fellow's fire as he slept.
(8) This guy arrives now, Mink does, (and) eats up the (other) fellow's salmon which he had been roasting.
(9) And he finished his (the old man's) food.

(10) And then Mink continues walking about.

After the first sentence, the two translations differ markedly. Most noticeable are the added adjectives and modifying phrases of the free translation, and the several details about how the Lushootseed people roast salmon. The protagonist's feelings are also expressed. The literal translation, in contrast, is devoid of these details for the style of syəyəhub is stark. Motives are never explained and scenes are never elaborated. The Lushootseed audience is intimately familiar with the personages in the old stories; therefore, the listeners fully understand their motives. The audience also knows thoroughly the culture and geography of the region where the stories take place. Such shared knowledge is not expressed in syəyəhub. Similarly, in daily life, much can be expressed tersely because everyone lives close together and, therefore, people are highly sensitive to each other's needs and moods.

On the other hand, in the old stories, the same statement is often made several times with altered syntax. Such repetition is tedious in English prose writing and, therefore, omitted in the free translations; but it is effective in Lushootseed recitation. In oral presentations, not only does the syntax vary, but also the rhythm and pitch. Often, stressed vowels are drawn out with a rising pitch. Alternatively, the raconteur sometimes rushes very quickly through a passage. Such changes add to the story's interest but are well nigh impossible to convey in writing.

Two other characteristics of syəyəhub difficult to render in English are songs and stylized speech. A large number of tales have one or more songs which constitute an important part of the story. Of course, lyrics can be translated but the melody is lacking and so are the special song syllables.

These syllables have no lexical meaning so they can not be translated; but in the songs they form an integral part of the mood.

In English oral traditions, there are special vocal mannerisms used to convey the inebriate, the idiot, the effeminate man, baby talk, and so forth. Such stylized speech is also used in Lushootseed to suggest certain personality traits. Characters having those traits are quoted in the old stories with appropriate speech changes. These too cannot be put into English writing for often the very sounds they entail are unknown in both English phonology and its orthographic representation.

Nevertheless, some features of syəyəhub narrative can be expressed in translation. For example, the reader will notice that over and over again, an event occurs four times or there are four participants. Four is the pattern number in Northern Lushootseed; it is as pervasive there as three is in Western cultures. In the southern Puget Sound region, however, patterns are fivefold, as occur in *Fly*, the only southern story in the collection. The Western influence in *The Legend of the Three Sisters* can be seen by the many sets of three instead of four.

The old stories often include in passing explanations for how things, especially animals, came to have the form they do. Although such explanations are usually peripheral to the plot, they are fun to learn about. The reader will also notice that a protagonist entering the story as a baby always grows to maturity astonishingly fast.

Finally, it should be observed that in their most traditional form, syəyəhub always begin with either of two formulae: "There was X" or "X dwelled (there)," where X is the name of the main character in the story. Traditional endings are equally laconic, simply noting "It is done now" or "X is out of breath now," This last is a humorous euphemism meaning that the protagonist has died.

These few features are part of what the typical Lushootseed storyteller always includes in a recitation. However, the listeners, too, have a role to play. As the story develops, the audience must call out "Haboo!" periodically. This exclamation encourages the raconteur. A more apt title for a collection of syəyəhub is hard to imagine.

HABOO

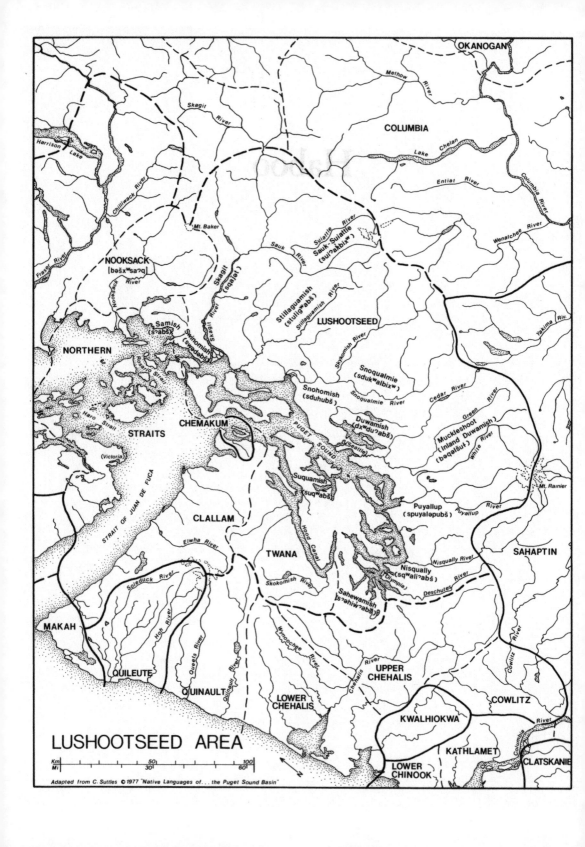

LUSHOOTSEED AREA

Km | 50 | 100
Mi | 30 | 60

Adapted from C. Suttles © 1977 "Native Languages of... the Puget Sound Basin"

OKANOGAN

COLUMBIA

Methow River

Skagit River

Lake Chelan

Entiat River

Wenatchee River

Columbia River

Harrison Lake

Chilliwack River

Fraser River

Mt. Baker

NOOKSACK
[bešxʷsaʔq]

Nooksack River

Skagit River (sqələt)

Sauk River

Suiattle River

Sauk-Suiattle
(suiʔabixʷ)

Stillaguamish
(stuligʷabš)

Stillaguamish River

LUSHOOTSEED

Yakima Riv.

Samish
(səabš)

Swinomish
(swədəbš)

NORTHERN

Rosario Strait

Skykomish River

Snoqualmie
(sduRʷalbixʷ)

Snoqualmie River

Cedar River

Green River

Haro Strait

STRAITS

CHEMAKUM

Snohomish
(sduhubš)

Duwamish
(dxʷduʔabš)
(Seattle)

Muckleshoot
(Inland Duwamish)
(baqəlšut)

White River

(Victoria)

PUGET SOUND

Mt. Rainier

STRAIT OF JUAN DE FUCA

CLALLAM

Suquamish
(suqʷabš)

Puyallup
(spuyaləpubš)

Puyallup River

Elwha River

Hood Canal

TWANA

Nisqually
(sqʷaliʔabš)
Dudmoia

Nisqually River

SAHAPTIN

MAKAH

Soleduck River

Hoh River

Skokomish River

Sahewamish
(seaqʷihwəbš)

Deschutes River

Cowlitz River

QUILEUTE

Queets River

Quinault River

Wynoochee River

Chehalis River

UPPER
CHEHALIS

COWLITZ

QUINAULT

LOWER
CHEHALIS

KWALHIOKWA

Columbia River

LOWER
CHINOOK

KATHLAMET

CLATSKANIE

Journey to the Sky and Back Down to the Earth

Told in English by Charley Anderson in 1954

A MAN WHO was from around the salt water somewhere was building a canoe. Every day he went to work on the canoe that he was building.

There were salmonberry bushes growing near this place where he was carving his canoe. One day as he worked he happened to glance toward the berry bushes, and he could see that the berries were forming. They were partly ripe now.

A few warm days later, he noticed that the berries were plump and yellowish-red. They were ripe enough to eat now. He thought, "I'm going to enjoy eating some of those berries." He put a hand up to pick the ripest ones. He couldn't quite reach them, so he stretched a little further. Suddenly, the salmonberries grabbed him and took him right up to the sky!

He couldn't go home. After a while, his people missed him and wondered what had become of him. They went to look for him but couldn't find him anywhere.

There was *one man* among them who had *special powers*. He could see into the future and he could foretell things. The villagers were worried and asked him to come and help them find the *respected canoe builder*. The man went to the place where the man had been working on his canoe. He stood there. After a while, he turned to the people and interpreted what he had received. He said, "It may be that he wished for these berries that are ripe, and it was those berries that took him up." The people listened quietly, and they believed what the man said to them.

The sky at that time was not as high as it is now. It was closer. The people thought, "If some of our strong people could shoot their arrows to the sky and the arrows stick up there, we could climb to the sky!"

All of the strong men, the big animals, shot their arrows at the sky. No! The arrows couldn't reach the sky. They just fell back to earth. These men were not strong enough. They gave up! The whole tribe felt defeated.

Little Chickadee came forward. His arms and legs were slender little bones. He stood there with his bow and arrow while the people explained to him what they were trying to do. Chickadee fastened his bowstring and attached an arrow, arched his bow a few times, aimed at the sky and shot his arrow upward. It stuck and stayed there. He fitted another arrow onto his bowstring and shot it into the butt of the arrow stuck in the sky. He repeated this until he had arrows all the way from the sky down to earth.

The people called their *special workers*. These workers spoke to the arrows, and these arrows grew into a big, strong tree. Woodpecker was then called. He pecked steps all around the tree. Yellowhammer followed behind and finished these steps. After this was done, all of the people lined up, and everybody just walked up this ladder to the sky! *Everybody went— animals, fish and birds*. They all went to look for the respected canoebuilder who had been taken.

It was very cold up there in the sky, and when Robin saw a fire, he went and sat as close as he could get to it. He stayed there while everyone else went searching for the man. Robin's chest got so warm as he sat there, it turned red; and that is why all robins have red chests to this day!

The people found a river up there with a fish trap down below. There were lots of people down by the fish trap. Beaver said to his people, "I am going to divert the attention of those people by drifting down toward their trap. While they are busy with me, you folks can be searching through their houses." Beaver slipped into the river and swam around the upper side of the trap. When they saw the stranger swimming near their fish trap, the people immediately rushed there and cornered and caught him. They carried him to a flat place. They thought that they had killed him. Beaver pretended to be dead while they began to skin him. He just lay there! The people searched the village houses.

Beaver began to worry as they skinned him half way, all the way to his backbone. "I *wish* my people would come!" Just as he was turned so that the skinners could begin on his other side, his people arrived! They had found the canoe builder! Beaver just rolled back over his hide, and it stuck to him.

All of them hurried and ran away from the villagers and their fish trap! They all started for home! Down the ladder they went. The big animals—Black Bear, Grizzly Bear, Elk and others—were halfway down when the ladder broke apart. The steps fell apart and dropped down. There were still many people up there in the sky, and they didn't know what to do.

Steelhead looked down and said to himself, "I am going to jump down. I won't get killed if I land." He *was a man at that time.* He just jumped down. When he landed, he landed in a clump of ironwood. He turned into a steelhead salmon when he landed. That is why the steelhead bones are so hard. No other fish has bones like steelhead.

Sucker was an Indian doctor at that time. He was up there. This Indian doctor turned and said to the people who were still up there with him, "Don't be afraid. All of you just get on my back. I'm going to jump down." *He was an Indian doctor!* They got on his back. When everyone was loaded there, he jumped down! He landed right in a big pile of fir bark. Now that is why Sucker has so many bones. That is also why there are bones of all shapes in Sucker's head: Eagle, Wolf, Fish Hawk, Bluejay and lots of others.* His head is not solid.

From that time, all of the Upper and Lower Skagit people instructed their children, *"You must not go and take berries when they are first ripe. You wait until the older people get the berries and pass it to the children."* They were afraid that the children might get sick from eating berries when they first begin to ripen.

That is the end.

* Elders used to be able to name every bone in Sucker's head and identify the animal it had come from.

Loon with Deer was Hunting Ducks with Bow and Arrow

*Told by Charley Anderson in English
at Everson, Washington, in 1954*

THIS LOON AND Deer were traveling together on a canoe. Loon was hunting, and Deer was going along. And Loon looked around and told Deer, "Deer, you see those people traveling on that canoe alongside that point?"

And Deer looked around. "No. No one travels. I never see anyone."

And Loon would see those people traveling—getting close—and ask Deer again, "You see those people traveling on the canoe?"

And Deer would look over and never see the people on the canoe.

And Loon thought to himself, "It's all right. The people won't bother me," The people were the Wolf people. And Loon thought about the knothole on the side of his canoe, close to the bottom, and he thought, "If the people come to us, I'll just go through that knothole near the bottom."

Well, these people were pretty close now, when Deer saw them. So Loon just went right through that knothole and dived into the water. And Deer didn't know what to do, just running back and forth in the canoe. So they took Deer along with them.

Well, these people went and camped on a sand bar. And, well, they were ready for bed and lying down, and these people said, "You sleep with us. Lie down with us."

And Doe said, "All right." So she lay down for a while.

And pretty soon this fellow told Doe, "You tell a story before we sleep."

And Deer said, "All right." Well, Deer said, "High Class, sleep soundly. High Class," And Deer repeated those words, the same words, all the time and never changed. Well, she would ask, "You awake yet?"

Well, this fellow never answered her, and she got up. The Deer got up and walked down to the canoe and got in the canoe and started out. Well, she got way out, and she started singing a song now:

"You are going to take
Your slave along here."

That Deer was way out now.

And she never knew that that canoe was tied to a long fishing line. And these people were pulling her back. When they got hold of that canoe, they just tore Deer up all to pieces.

And Flounder, she was there, a person. Ah, she had no chance to get any of the meat. And she just grabbed Deer's guts, a whole bunch, and she threw it over her shoulder and jumped into the water. That's why Flounder turned into a fish now, because she had Deer's guts over her shoulder. Flounders have guts under the back skin.

And that's why Deer are caught easy now.

That's the end of the story.

The Basket Ogresses Chase Coyote

Told in English by Charley Anderson
at Everson, Washington, in 1954

THIS COYOTE WAS traveling, and he saw some children playing. Coyote asked them, "Whose children are you? What are your mother's and father's names?" The children couldn't understand him. They couldn't speak. Their mouths just went, "Mmmmmmmp, Mmmmmmm, Mmmmmmm, Mmmmmp." He couldn't understand these children, so he killed them and he went on away. Yeah.

Ɂáxʷadus. There were two sisters; they followed the tracks that were Coyote's. Pretty soon Coyote saw the Ɂáxʷadus coming. He ran. Then he came to a place. It was a rock by the beach, and there was a hole in it, way, way inside. The hole wasn't big enough for a big person to go in, but it was big enough for Coyote to crawl through.

Well, he stayed there. He would peek out, and there were those two Ɂáxʷadus right there, sitting on each side of the entry. He stayed inside. Well, he didn't know what to do now. He was hungry, and there was no water to drink. He was getting so bony. Just skin and bone now.

Well, he thought to himself, "I'll make believe that there are lots of people who live here. I'm going to holler to my neighbors across the river." He hollered to his neighbors, "Oh, you, my friends, tomorrow we move down the river." After that he hollered and pretended that his friends were answering him from across the river. He kind of said, low, "Oh, all right. Yes." Yeah.

Well, those ʔáxʷadus gave up waiting for that Coyote to come out. They found out that there are lots of people in there who are going to move down the river tomorrow. Well, when Coyote would move, all of his bones rattled. It sounded like dry poles {used for shades inside the house}, and that's what the ʔáxʷadus thought. But it was Coyote's bones rattling. Coyote went to the opening and peeked out. He saw that the ʔáxʷadus were gone now. They had given up. He was in there all by himself. He went out.

Oh, when he got out, he wished for a drink of water. He ran down to the water and put his face down to drink. He saw something coming from under the water. It was a real tough-looking animal coming to bite him. He got scared and stepped back. He was so thirsty. After a while he tried again. He went slow, slow, so he could get a drink of water. He put his face close to that water, and he saw the animal coming from under the water, ready to bite him! He ran back again, he was so scared. Four times he did that; then he thought to himself, "I wonder if it is my shadow that I see under the water?" He went and drank, and he found out. "It's my shadow that looks so tough—just bones with teeth sticking out!" He had gone without food for such a long time. He drank that water.

That is the end of the story.

Wolf Brothers Kill
Elk and Beaver

Told in English by Charley Anderson in 1954

A LONG TIME ago in what is now called the Myth Age, *four Wolf brothers lived there.* One day the eldest Wolf called his brothers together and told them, "I hear that there is something very bad going on. That Elk who lives there under the water is killing people who travel on the river. That's wrong! We must do something about it. We must kill that Elk so people can travel without being bothered,"

Before they all went out to kill Elk, each of the brothers made his own knife. The knives varied in size. The eldest had the biggest, and the smallest knife belonged to the youngest brother.

After their knives were made, the brothers set out to find Elk. They traveled a long way. Suddenly they saw something in the water. It was as tall as a tree—but, no, it's not a tree! They look closely and they can see that it is a huge set of horns!

The eldest brother called his brothers to him and instructed them: "We shall put a log in the water above the Elk; then our youngest brother will ride the log down the river. When the Elk swallows the log he'll get inside of the Elk." He told his little brother, "When you get inside of that Elk, you take my knife and cut the Elk's heart out."

As the log drifted down the river, Elk saw it coming. He opened his mouth and swallowed the whole thing. When little brother got accustomed to the dark place inside of Elk, he thought about his oldest brother's instructions. He could hear Elk's heart thumping, and he began to walk until he could feel it; then he began to cut. He cut only about one quarter, and his knife melted and the handle fell off. He grabbed the knife of an older brother. He managed to cut about one half way before again the knife melted. He took the next brother's knife and cut at Elk's heart. One more quarter he cut before the knife melted away. Now he took his own little knife and he cut Elk's heart right off!

The three older brothers worried and waited for their little brother to get back. The oldest brother began to cry as he worried that his baby brother might have been killed by Elk. The other two quickly comforted him when they watched the huge horns topple and fall over. Soon they saw something that made them all laugh. Mink bobbed up out of the water after the horns of Elk toppled over. As he ran by them, they could see that he was bald-headed! Unknown to the four Wolf brothers, Mink had jumped on top of the logs and floated down the river. Mink hoped that this would kill Elk when he swallowed so many logs. Elk just swallowed all of the logs with Mink riding on top. It didn't hurt Elk one little bit! But it was so hot down inside Elk's stomach, it burned all of the hair off Mink's head before he had a chance to get out!

After Elk was dead, the eldest Wolf called his brothers to him and said, "We are going to make spearheads from Elk's horns. Each will be different. I will make four barbs in mine, and each of you will put one less on yours. You, my youngest brother, you will have only one notch on your spear."

When they had finished making their spears, the oldest brother said, "Now we shall go and look for that big Beaver that's somewhere in the lake. That Beaver has ten tails!"

The brothers searched until finally they found the Beaver's house at the edge of the lake. He had a long deep waterway he swam through when he left his home. The eldest Wolf again instructed his brothers: "Each of you space your spear poles in the Beaver's waterway. I will have mine nearest to his house so that I can warn each of you when he comes out."

The brothers poked their spear poles at Beaver's house until finally he started swimming toward his waterway. Eldest brother hollered at the youngest one and told him to use his spear on the Beaver. Little Wolf saw this Beaver, and he said, "No, that's not the one!" He let it go on by. Four of these Beaver came out, and he just let them go on by because he knew that they were not *the* one! Pretty soon a great, huge Beaver came out. The eldest Wolf tried to holler at his brothers, but he was so scared he lost his voice. He opened his mouth to holler, but no sound came forth.

The youngest brother saw the Beaver and he knew: *"This is the one!"* He grabbed the spearhead with four barbs—he speared the Beaver, and the spear just broke right off. It couldn't hold. It wasn't strong enough. He used each of the spears made by his brothers, and none of them would hold. The last spear was his, with just one notch. When he thrust the spear into Beaver, it went deep, but it didn't stop Beaver. He just kept on going.

Wolf held on to the pole. As Beaver pulled him along. Wolf grabbed ahold of a big tree and held on tightly. The big tree fell over, roots and all. Now little Wolf tried to let go of his spear pole, but his hands just stuck to it. He couldn't let go! He grabbed on to a big rock as Beaver pulled him along. The big rock just rolled over, and Beaver didn't stop. This Beaver kept going, pulling him along until the stream joined the big Columbia River! Little brother Wolf despaired! Nothing would stop this huge Beaver!

Honeysuckle and bú?bx̌əb* heard about their grandson's trouble. bú?bx̌əb prepared to help his grandson. He positioned himself downstream. He tied belts around his body, his waist and his chest, and he had himself ready. Honeysuckle had himself wrapped all around the trees way back in the forest, and he stood waiting to help his grandson who was in trouble. When they saw him coming toward them, the old gentlemen hollered, "Grab ahold of us. Grandson! We will help you! Grab ahold of us!"

Young Wolf heard them and he saw how old they were. Old people didn't really have much strength. He pitied them, and he didn't grab ahold of them as he went by. Three times he passed them.

When they saw him go by for the third time, the old men ran ahead to the bend in the river and there they waited for their young grandson. When he came near, again they hollered, "Grab ahold. Grandson! We will help you!"

Young Wolf was feeling pretty worried by now, so he thought, "Maybe I should try these old fellows." As soon as he grabbed Honeysuckle, there

---

* bú?bx̌əb is a slender green reed (scouring rush) which the Salish people used as sandpaper to smooth wood.

was a squeaking noise way back among the trees in the forest, and búʔbx̌əb made a funny noise as his belts all tightened around him.

Beaver stopped! He couldn't move the two old men who were helping their grandson, Wolf!

Wolf found big round sticks which Beaver had chewed off. He took one of these sticks and clubbed Beaver over the head with it. Killed him! Then he said, "The coming generation is going to club Beaver like this, with these sticks he has chewed on!" Now Wolf fixed Beaver into a bundle, and he put him on his back and he walked. He packed Beaver back to his other brothers.

The eldest brother was crying! He thought his baby brother had drowned! When he saw that he was well and safe, he gathered all of his brothers around him and again gave them instructions. He said, "We are going to hire Hummingbird and Bumblebee. We shall cut this Beaver meat into little pieces. Hummingbird and Bumblebee will take the pieces all over the country and plant them so that we will have Beaver all over our country."

So in every stream of water and on all of the lakes, Hummingbird and Bumblebee put little chunks of the Beaver meat. Beaver then grew there, and that is why we have beaver all over!

That is the end of the story.

Boil and Hammer
Are Living There

Told in English by Charley Anderson
at Everson, Washington, in 1954

BOIL AND HAMMER were sisters. This Boil had long hair, braided down. And she went out and picked berries every day, every day. The two sisters, Boil and Hammer, went out and picked berries.

Every day they went out and came home. That's all they lived on—berries, berries, every day. One day they were going home, and Hammer, she was walking ahead, and Boil came behind and had the berries on her back. So Hammer got home and she waited there. And her sister never showed up. Well, she worried.

So she walked back on the trail. Well, she came to find her sister's hair—just her hair, two braids lying on the trail. Those sharp things, the fir needles, one must have dropped on top of Boil's head. And it busted—just busted! She had no bones, just a braid.

Yeah, Hammer felt bad and cried and cried going home and got into their house, and she stayed there. Yeah. She quit crying. "Well, I'll go down the river and wash my face." So she went down to the river and washed. She had pretty beads on.

Her foot slipped, and she rolled down into the river. She was just a rock, anyhow. So Hammer, she got drowned.

That is the end of the story.

Basket Ogress

Told by Louise {tsi sqʷúx̌ʷaʔɬ} Anderson,
Upper Skagit–Samish, in 1962

IN THE TIME of legends, it seems that the children were sent to gather together by the shore of the salt water.

When they arrived there they were hungry, so they built a fire to roast their salmon. They roasted their salmon. When it was cooked, they divided it into little pieces, one for each child. Little Hunchback was given the tail. He was told, "The tail part will be your share, Little Hunchback."

Little Hunchback felt so insulted. He hollered, "Come on. Ogress, come on! I have just been given the tail of the roasted salmon."

The frightened children said, "Be quiet, be quiet, Little Hunchback! Be quiet! The Basket Ogress might come here to us!"

Again they roasted a salmon. Four times they roasted their salmon, and always it was just the tail that was given to Little Hunchback. Now he thought: *I am going to holler!*

"Come on down to the water, Basket Ogress. These little children just give me the tail!"

"Be quiet, be quiet! Be quiet. Little Hunchback! The Basket Ogress might come to us."

"Let her come!"

"If she comes, you will be the first one that she takes, Little Hunchback!"

"Oh, no. I will always be on top!" Then he hollered again: "Come on, Basket Ogress, come on down towards the water!"

Again the frightened children pleaded, "Don't, don't call the Basket Ogress—she might come!"

Suddenly they heard something making noise. It was Basket Ogress' cane. She had deer hooves tied there, and they rattled as she walked.

"See there! Basket Ogress is coming!"

"No, no! Don't call her! No!"

They were grabbed. Put into a big clam basket! It was on the back of the Basket Ogress. She put in another child. Little Hunchback squirmed around, always getting himself up to the top as the Ogress threw more children into her basket. This clam basket of Ogress' was made entirely of snakes. Just snakes!

There were eleven children, including Little Hunchback. There were eleven.

She arrived.

She sang as she happily built a hot fire and placed rocks there to heat. When the rocks were hot, the Basket Ogress was pushed! Then she sang a different song:

Take me out of the fire,
Children, please!
Take me out of the fire,
Children, please!
Take me out of the fire,
Children, please!

The children answered, "We *are* taking you out of the fire. We are taking you out of the fire, but the flames and the rocks are so hot!"

"Put out the fire, children. Put out the fire."

"No, no, Basket Ogress! We can't get it out. We have tried in vain to put it out!"

Basket Ogress again sang her request four times:

Remove me from the fire,
Children, please!
Remove me from the fire,
Children, please!
Remove me from the fire,
Children, please!

Remove me from the fire,
Children, please!

The happy children danced around as she sang. They sang in reply:

We are removing you,
Basket Ogress—

"But we can't seem to manage to get you out!"

The fire burned until it went out. They tried in vain to get the Basket Ogress out.

Little Hunchback ran. He went down to the water. He got there. He wanted to be in the bow of the canoe.

"No, no, Little Hunchback. No! You get in the middle, get in the stern." But no. They didn't get Little Hunchback on board. They went where they were going.

Little Hunchback threw rocks at them. He'd fix them. Their paddles would break!

The children arrived where they had come from.

"What did you children do? What did you do with your younger brother?" They were all women at that place. There were no men among them.

"We left Little Hunchback because he wouldn't listen to us when we tried to stop him."

"Oh, okay. It was all right that you left him."

Now his grandfather went out looking for Little Hunchback. He put his grandson on board and they traveled through the swamp grass and reeds that grew there. When he arrived home he asked the children, "Why did you leave your younger brother?"

They answered, "Well, it was because he called the Basket Ogress and she would have burned us. That is why we got angry with him and we left him!"

That is the end of the story.

Legend of the Seasons
(All Year Round Story)

Told by Emma Conrad at Burlington, Washington,
to Thom Hess on March 28, 1963

THIS IS A story of how things were a long time ago.

People lived in a village with their houses side by side. This was a good way that the people lived, side by side. The leader of this village had a young daughter. A family who lived in another house had a young son. As time passed, these two young people grew fond of each other, and the young man spoke of marrying the girl who was the daughter of the leader of their village.

The girl's family disapproved strongly, because the young man's family was very poor. Their stations in life were not equal. The girl's father was the Head Man. This Head Man told his daughter that he forbade her marriage to someone who was not her equal. The girl ignored the words of her father!

The father took some cedar, and he made a box. He made it large enough for two people to be put inside. He made it watertight. Now he took his son-in-law and his daughter and put them into the box and nailed it closed. He then put it on a canoe and took it offshore. He put it overboard: he wanted the box to sink. It floated!

The box turned around and around as it floated. Sometimes it would drift ashore, and then the water would come up and float it again. It floated like this for one moon.

Now, there was a woman who lived way down near the ocean. She lived all by herself on a little island. The beach was covered with pebbles, and

the area upland was covered with green foliage. The box drifted to this island, and it landed right below where the woman was. The box landed there and was there for some time.

The woman spoke to her servants. She had three of them. One was her cook, one cleaned the house, and one washed the dishes. They were her servants. She had lived there from the beginning of the world. She had never traveled anywhere else. Now she spoke to her young people, saying, "Let us go for a walk down by the water's edge." she carried her little axe along as the four of them walked along the beach. The beach was covered with small pebbles.

Suddenly they saw a box! It was on the beach. The woman spoke to her young people: "What is that on the beach?" They went near it and could see that it was indeed a box. When the woman got there she turned to her young women and said, "This is a very nice box. Let us save it. Let us open it and find out more about it." She took her little hatchet and opened the box: then they saw the two people inside. They saw the man and the woman. She said, "We had better take this man home." They put the woman back inside the box.

They took the man home and put him to work for them. They made him their husband. The man had things turn out very nicely for him in this place that he came to.

He had been there for some time, and now, the wild blackberries were getting ripe (about July). The woman turned to her servants and said, "Let us take this man back home so that we can see his people."

They got ready for their journey by water. He didn't know it, but they had a ship, and this is what they all got aboard. After they were all on board, the woman took four nuts, and she put them into the man's pockets. She put two into one pocket, the youngest one and the eldest. The middle one she put into another pocket. Then she said that she wanted to return him to his wife. The man argued against it until he had to give up.

He took the youngest one that he had been given, and he rolled it. It rolled, then stood up. There it was, a person! They couldn't see for a long time, because this woman was shining so brightly. After a long time, they could see her: she was a very nice-looking woman.

The Head Man looked at her, and he said, "My daughter is still better. You had better take her back."

The young man took the eldest nut, and he let it go. It rolled on the floor and then stood up. The same thing happened again. The people couldn't see her for a long time, because she was so brightly shining. When their eyes could finally see her, they saw that she was even prettier than the other girl.

Still the old man didn't give up. He argued, "My daughter is still prettier than this woman." The young man argued, too, until he gave up.

Now he took the cook, and he rolled her. She stood up. She was prettier yet!

The man lost his wives because he made them visible. He made them visible the time that he was supposed to. The woman took her servants home!

Now the young man didn't know how he was going to manage to get his wife back. He just felt sad, and he began to walk. He walked toward the east. He walked toward the east. He walked until he arrived at his first destination.

The people were playing a game that they had been playing since the beginning of the world. The game was called sbəbiʔ. They rolled a hoop from the top of this mountain. It was a bluish mountain. This is where the people were playing. They rolled the hoop downhill. They had little spears. The one who could put a spear through the hoop before it reached the bottom of the mountain was the winner. They had been playing this game from the beginning of time, and no one had been able to put a spear through the hoop. They played all year long and then started through another year.

This was the place where the man who was walking arrived. He just observed those who were playing, and he turned away.

He continued walking. He arrived at a land far away. Again he came to people who were also on a mountain, but this was a good mountain. The people sat on this mountain. They had a pipe which they smoked. They just smoked this long pipe. The pipe reached to the foot of the mountain. When they smoked, the earth was covered with clouds.

This is where the man arrived. He visited there. He observed what the old {men were} doing before he left {them}.

Again he went. He went to a land far away, and he came to three young men. Their eldest brother had left them; he had died. Their brother had had a very good garment, and it was this garment which they had placed there high on this mountain. It was this garment which they were arguing about. Each one was claiming it for himself.

"I am going to be the one to take my older brother's garment!"

Another one would say, "No! I am going to be the one to take it."

They had been doing this since their brother died. From the beginning of the world they had been doing this, until the day came when the man who was walking arrived there where they were. He came to the ones who were arguing about that garment. The young men told him what they were doing.

Then he said to the young men, "I shall tell you what to do in order to get the garment of your brother. It is not good for you to be just arguing! I shall take this big ball and roll it, and you will follow it. The one who gets it before it reaches the bottom of the mountain is the one who will win the garment."

The young men went running behind the rolling ball. None of them could manage to get it before it landed at the bottom. One took it, and they climbed back up the mountain, arguing.

"I am the one who got the ball."

"No! It was I who got it!"

They were saying this until they got to the top, where the man was waiting for them. He told them, "None of you got the ball. I shall roll it again, and you will chase it." Again he took it and he rolled it. It rolled down the mountain, and the men ran behind it until it reached the bottom of the mountain, and no one had been able to get it. One took it, and they all returned, arguing.

"I am the one who got it."

And another would say, "No! I am the one who got it."

They kept saying this until they again reached the top of the mountain, where he was waiting for them. Again they were told: "Not one of you got it; I am going to roll it again." He rolled it again, and again the young men went running after it.

Now he took the garment. He put it on. It just fit him exactly. He took it off and laid it down.

The men returned, arguing until they reached the top. This is the third time now. When it came to the fourth time, he said to them, "I am going to roll it, and you will chase it. This will be the fourth time. The one who gets it will win the garment." The young men went chasing the ball for the fourth time. The man took the garment and *he* put it on. The young men ran to the bottom of the mountain: not one of them managed to get the ball. One went and took it, and they brought it back, arguing until they arrived with it. The man was nowhere. He wasn't there, and the garment wasn't there!

The eldest one said, "Where did he go? Where is the garment?"

Now the youngest one said, "Oh, I've thought for a long time that he was going to take the garment. That's why he had us do what we were doing."

But *he* is there, listening. He has on the garment. Just as soon as someone puts on the garment, that person becomes invisible. You would not be visible if you put on the garment! This is the reason that they had been arguing about it. Each of them wanted to have it. Then there they were just talking, and he left them.

Again he went. He had the garment on as he went. He walked to the land far away. The cold weather was coming. He walked until he came to a house. It was not a very big house. He went and looked to see who was there. All he could see was an old woman lying face down on her little bed.

He spoke to the woman, and she said to him, "You are not to continue on your journey. You are to stay here. My grandsons are powerful. My grandsons are powerful. If you were to travel now and you were to meet them, you would freeze. My four grandsons are powerful!" She said to him then, "I shall take you and put you behind me and cover you up."

There he was, face down until the eldest one came. He was the one who came. The house didn't get very cold as he came near. The old woman said, "My oldest grandson is coming. My oldest grandson will arrive, and we will be just shaking from the cold when he arrives."

The grandson came to the door and came on inside. He said, "Hmmm. I smell the smell of a human being!"

The old woman replied, "And where would a human being come from? I am all alone here!"

He went then. Then he went and stood there where he was, this *Cold*.

The man was there for one long moon.

Then another grandson arrived. It was still colder. The old woman again said to the man, "The next eldest one is coming." She said, "He is the coldest!" She almost freezes as he approaches. She huddles there, face down, with her blanket wrapped around her face. She shakes with cold as her grandson comes.

When he arrives, he says also, "Hmmmmm, I smell the smell of a human being!"

The old woman replied, "And where would a human being come from? I am all alone here."

He went. He placed himself there where he is when summer comes. This is the second one now.

The man is still there. He is waiting for another moon to come.

He came. He is the third one. He came. The old woman said to the man, "My grandson is coming!" He came there. It got very cold. It gets very cold when he comes. They call it "*Sides-stick*" because this moon is mighty cold, and things stick together: bark to a tree and paddles to the side of a canoe.

After he arrives, it is a shorter time until he comes in the door. He also says, "Hmmmmm. I smell a human being!"

The old woman replied, "No. Where would a human being come to me from? I am all alone."

He went where he went. There he stayed.

Now this man waited for one moon. He was there for four moons. The old woman said to him,. "My youngest grandson is coming now." She gets up when it gets warm.

This grandson's work is everything that his brothers have frozen. This person fixes everything. They come and tell that their fingers are broken, their heads are broken, their ears, their feet. This is the reason they come. They have been overcome by the ice! Now the cold months pass. It gets cold when they walk the earth. The cold weather falls, the wind, the snow, the ice! The ice floats on the river from the way these men are, and they pass.

Then the world gets good again: the month of their youngest brother. He comes, and he fixes up the world. He helps those with cut-off fingers, cut-off feet, cut-off ears, heads cut off from the frozen ways of these three men. Now their younger brother is nice. Warm! He fixes everything up in this world. Now the world gets stronger; it gets good again when the youngest one comes. Shortly after he begins to work, the world gets good again. He arrives then where his brothers and his grandmother are. She is always there, and this is where they all return.

The grandmother said to the man, "My grandson has arrived. It is getting very warm!" She said to the one that she had covered up, "You had better get up now. The earth is warm now." The man got up. The older ones, who had come in before, just looked at him. They didn't say anything as he came forward when the earth became warm.

That one arrived. He also said, "Hmmmmm, I smell the smell of a human being."

The old woman replied, "No! Where would a person come from? I am all alone where I am."

He came in, and he saw the man there. They found each other. Now they were good friends. They talked together. They talked about the way his brothers were, what they did when they went traveling and things got cold. They froze everything. They freeze people to death from the cold, from the ice, from the snow that piles up high. This is what he tells the man. He says, "This is what I have been working on, and that is why I am so tired when I come home, fixing up everything that they have killed." Now he asked the young man where he was going.

The young man replied, "I am looking for my wife whom I lost. There were four. Three were servants. She is the one I am looking for!"

This one said to him, "Oh yes, there is a woman over there. She is going to get married. She is going to marry after a while. She is going to feed the people at midnight. She will feed lots of people." He told this man, "You had better go fast, because she is getting married today, and she is going to feed the people at midnight."

Now the man will travel. He is going to look for his wife. He has four wives. One works in the house, one cooks, one washes dishes—this is what the youngest one does—these servants of this woman.

The man traveled. He walked from morning until midnight before he arrived where his wife was going to get married. He looked at those inside. He had on *the garment*! No one could see him. There were many people. They were eating the food provided by this woman who was getting married. No one could see him. There were many people. They were eating the food provided by this woman who was getting married. There he was, and he stood behind his wife.

The man that she was to marry was there, and they were talking to each other. Suddenly she said, (*He* had arrived, and he had taken his wife's herb-tea and drunk it), the woman said, "Oh, you didn't give me any herb-tea." Her servant came and took her cup and filled it.

The woman again talked with the one she was going to marry. The man took her herb-tea and drank it. She kept on talking with her husband-to-be. Again she missed her herb-tea. This is the second time! She said, "You haven't given me any herb-tea! I called for some, and still I have no herb-tea!"

Her servant replied, "I gave you some herb-tea, but you didn't drink it."

It happened for the third time, and she began to think that it might be something that her husband was doing, if he is the one doing this. Some herb-tea is poured for her. She talks with her fiance; they never stop talking together. Now for the fourth time she looks at her herb-tea, and her cup is empty! "You still haven't given me any herb-tea, and I have called for some many times now!"

She stood up now and went to her bedroom. She looked for her long-range lens. She came back out and looked through them. She looked around, trying to see. She returned to her bedroom. She brought out another pair. She looked and she looked! No! She can't see him. She returned that pair and brought out another. This is the third one. Again she looked: still she couldn't see him. She returned that pair and brought a bigger one. Now she saw her husband. There is her husband standing behind her, drinking her herb-tea.

She immediately sent the fiance away, and she ran to her husband and hugged him!

That is the end!*

---

* Compared with "Legend of the Seasons" by Harry Moses (p. 107), this version seems to leave out a couple of explanatory passages. Consult and compare them both for clarifications.

Fly

Told by Annie Daniels in Southern Lushootseed
at Puyallup in 1952

FLY WAS LIVING there when he heard about a gathering that was going to take place. Then he went. He traveled by water. He paddled with his hands. Along the way he met the Changer, who was going around making things the way they are now.

The Changer told Fly, "ʔaš, don't do that, don't paddle with your hands."

"Oh, honorable sir, if I pick up a stick to use, it hits me."

"ʔaš, that's not right." The Changer used the power of his mind on the paddle stick, and Fly was able to pick it up. Now Fly and the Changer went together. Now they paddled. The stick had been split in half to make a paddle, and it had died. Future generations would now know how to do this and take wood for paddles. The wood would no longer hit them back if they did this.

Fly said, "Oh, I am a poor person, yet I heard about this gathering and decided to go." Fly went. Yes, indeed. He arrived where a lot of people were living. He made a house next to them. As he looked around, he saw lots of cedar trees. He went and chopped at the base of some (until he could split off a section the same way that he split sticks to kill them for paddles. He gouged out the bottom until he could put in wedges to split off a large section.) He knocked this down. He began to carve it out, for it was large enough to make a canoe. Yes, that's what he did. He made a canoe.

While he was working, he heard a baby crying. The child cried, and then it stopped. It would cry for a time, and then it would stop. The baby, wrapped in a cradleboard, had been hidden by its mother. Fly kept hearing the baby for a long time. On the fifth day, he went over to look for it. Oh, it was a fine child that had been wrapped up and thrown away into the brush.

Fly went home and said to his wife, "You could pretend to have a child, and we could save the baby that is wrapped in the cradleboard."

The woman said, "All right."

Then Fly made a birthing hut outside {to make it look like his wife was having the baby}. He went and got the child and took it inside the hut to his wife, who nursed it. She heated her breasts, and then she was able to nurse it. When daylight came, people said of her, "Oh, it looks like the wife of Fly had a baby, but it seems to be much older than a newborn." They went closer and looked at it: "Oh, that woman's baby is already a child."

Fly already had a daughter named qʷəcx̌ʷaʔ. The new child grew very quickly. Time passed, and he grew older. Fly made him a bow; he made him arrows. Now the boy went off shooting. His sister, qʷəcx̌ʷaʔ went along with him.

When they were deep in the woods, she acted silly and said, "Now shoot me in the hand."

The boy said, "Oh, no, you would be hurt!"

She insisted, "Shoot me in the hand."

"Oh, no, you would be hurt. I won't shoot you. Your father would scold me for that."

She said a third time, "Oh, go ahead and shoot at my hand."

"No, I will not shoot you," he said.

She kept this up until the fifth time, when he shot her in the hand. Then his older sister screamed, "Owee, owee, owee! I was shot by the one who was discarded and then retrieved, the foundling that my parents pretended was their own!"

Her mother heard the screaming: "Oh, that daughter of mine is all mouth!" She hurried into the brush and scolded her daughter. "What is your younger brother doing, that you quarrel with him?"

The boy was no longer a little child, and his sister's words hurt him. He lay spreadeagled on the ground and cried and cried. He was off by himself. His mother and others called to him, but he would not come home. No! He lay on the ground crying until they stopped looking for him and calling his name. When night came, he got up and ran away. He ran toward the east, where the sun usually is. Yes, indeed, he ran. So Fly was without a son: he ran away, and they couldn't find him.

He kept traveling until he heard someone singing. "Oh, how nicely the woman sings!" Before he realized it, there was a nice woman standing beside him. He had never seen her before. He said, "Oh, Aunt, I want to hear you sing some more."

"Oh, no. You would suffer misfortune if we sang."

He insisted, "Oh, but I really like your song."

"Oh, no. You would certainly meet with misfortune if we were to sing."

Still he continued to coax this woman to sing. After a long time, her younger sister appeared and told the woman, "Oh, go ahead and sing, even if our nephew will meet with misfortune. He wants to hear you!"

The woman began to sing. Immediately the boy lost his senses. She sang:

"We belong to heat, we belong to heat."

Now the earth began to burn. The boy ran now. He asked the rock, "What do you do when you burn?"

Rock said, "I snap and pop."

He asked the water, "What do you do when you get hot?"

"Oh, I boil."

He asked the road. Road said, "Oh, I spread apart."

He asked everything. Finally, he came to the fir tree, and he asked it now, "What do you do when you burn?"

"Oh, I just burn a little bit on the bottom." Then the boy climbed up into the branches of that tree, way up until he was at the top. He had five arrows. He decided to use his five arrows to make a ladder to the High World. He used all five, but he was still just short of the sky. He was near the High World, but his arrows alone were not adequate to reach it. He took his bow and added it to his ladder, and he was able to get up higher. He dug a hole through the ground of the High World and climbed in. He reached down for his bow and arrows. Then he covered over the hole and walked away.

He walked far. He didn't eat anything. He saw sweet, ripe berries along the road, but this world was strange to him, so he resisted: he just looked at the berries as he passed. Suddenly, he saw an elk coming, and the earth behind it became brightly lit. He moved out of the way, and the elk passed him as it went. The light was still far away, but growing brighter. Suddenly, he saw that it was a person coming closer. It was a man chasing the elk. The man came up to the boy and said, "Say, my in-law, why didn't you shoot my game?"

The boy was confused and uncertain what to answer. "Oh, the elk didn't pass here long ago at all; you can still get it." This man was Day, and he claimed the boy for his daughters. He gave the boy meat, and they talked.

Day said, "I have five daughters, who will all become your wives when you get to my home." Daylight got up and went on chasing the elk. Toward evening, he was close enough to get a good view and took a shot.

Meanwhile, the boy saw someone else coming, walking along on a trail of dead cedar bark. The person came closer, and he saw that it was a man who was as skinny as a skeleton. The boy stepped aside, and the man just passed by. The boy went on. Oh, it was dark under the trees now when it was night.

When morning came, the boy walked again. He walked all day until it again became night. He waited, and again morning came. {In that twilight before full dawn, suddenly he met a person.} This was Night, who said, "Say, in-law, why didn't you shoot my game when he went past?"

The boy did not understand: "All I saw was a very skinny person going by."

"Oh, that was my game that you saw," Night answered. They visited for a while; then Night gave the boy some meat. It was meat for the dead. The child did not eat it. He looked around and saw a root that looked edible, and he just ate that. Except for the food, he and Night got along well and parted friends, exchanging bows and arrows. {Night had taken his from the dead, but the boy did not know this.} As he finished eating, Night warned him, "Do not go where you will be hidden. Stay on the light-colored paths beside creeks, where the sunlight is reflected. Do not go on a path that hides you."

The boy went on. Yes, indeed. Then he came to a fork in the path. He was uncertain what to do. He decided to go along the bright trail for a distance, then return to the fork and take the dark trail and follow it for a while and then come back. He did this for a long time, and nothing happened to him, so he was happy. {He did not understand that Day, being bright himself, used the dark path, while Night needed the light path to see his way clearly.}

Finally, the boy took the light path and followed it until he got to a bluff and paused. {He heard voices and realized that the bluff was really the roof of a house. He heard women inside and looked down. Through the smoke outlet he could see that there were young women inside. He watched them. The youngest of these sisters was very smart and realized that the boy was standing on the roof. He was expected. When the time was right, the youngest pretended to notice that the boy was there,} and she said to her older sister, "Oh, your husband has arrived!"

Then they all knew. They went outside and called him to come down. They took him and heated water. They bathed him, dried him off and massaged him with oil from the dead. Oh, the man stank from the stink-oil of the dead! They offered him meat, but he would not eat it. Instead he again ate more roots. {He finished eating, and the girls got him ready for bed.}

{There were five sisters, and he had met the youngest four. These were active and alive, but the oldest one did not join them. She was more mature and stayed in a coffin-like box or storage basket. He spent the night with the younger four, leaving the oldest in her container. Morning came, and each of the sisters got up and went hunting. When the youngest one left, the boy, now a man, thought of the oldest sister. He decided that it would be only fair to take her out to "play" that morning. He opened the container, and the woman woke up. He took her out, and they laughed together until they heard someone coming. The visitor was named čəx̌qapəd, Split Foot. By the time he got to the door, the boy had put the oldest sister back in her container and fastened the bindings on it. Poor Split Foot! He would never leave there alive!}

Meanwhile, Day had arrived home and asked his daughters, "Did your husband arrive yet?"

"No!"

Day was worried. "Maybe he took the wrong turn and ended up with the daughters of Night." The Daylight sisters grew angry at this and decided to raid the daughters of Night. The daughters of Night barred the door, so the Daylight sisters had to stay outside boiling with anger.

The boy saw them: "Oh! These must be the good women Day advised me about. How brightly they shine!" But the Daylight women went home, leaving the boy feeling very sad.

He stayed with the Night women for five more days. The fifth morning he told one of his wives, "I think I will walk around a bit outside; don't be afraid, I won't go anywhere." Just as soon as he went out, he ran toward the fork in the path. He got there, and then he ran until he reached the daughters of Day. The Daylight sisters opened the door as he approached. He saw them,— oh, he saw them! Day called out, "Your husband has arrived!" They warmed water to bathe him. They rubbed his body all over with a fragrant herb.

While this was happening, the daughters of Night arrived. They had killed the one who had come to their house when the boy and the oldest sister had been playing. Now they stood outside the Daylight sisters' home, still holding the foot of the corpse, and just boiling with rage.

The Day women said to the boy, "Now you see how they are, don't take them again; they are no good at all."

The boy had made up his mind that he would not: "Oh, it is such a good place that I have come to."

His father-in-law came home with the elk he had killed. They had a good meal. Yes, indeed.

And now his wife, the youngest one, said she was pregnant. {The husband was very pleased, telling the others he was to be a father. The other sisters knew better and told him that the youngest was just fooling him. That made him homesick. He remembered the hole he had crawled through and went out to find it. He couldn't pin-point it, so he made another. He scratched the earth to make a hole. He could see his mother down below him. She had had another baby boy. He felt very sad.}

While he was away, the older sisters went to the youngest: "Why do you upset your husband? What do you quarrel with him about?"

"Oh, I don't quarrel with him, he just feels sad all the time. He just feels bad."

The sisters waited for a long time for a proper answer, but they never got one. Then they left. The husband asked, "Oh, what were your sisters doing here? It sounded like they were scolding you."

His wife put him off, too.

He said, "I went out for a walk and found a hole in the earth. I looked down and saw my mother, and I now have a younger brother."

His wife said, "Oh, why didn't you mention this before? If you are homesick, my father can return us to your home quickly."

They waited for Day to come home. When he did, the daughter told him. Day said, "You could get home fast. I can get you there in no time at all." The man was pleased and prepared to leave. The Daylight people gave him gifts to take along. A piece of goat hair blanket was cut for him. They gave him dentalia, food and meat; he tenderly held these gifts.

Then a ladder was lowered to the earth below. It ended just where his people went to dip their water. Soon his younger brother came to get water. The man said, "Oh, come shake hands with me, for I am your older brother who walked away from here. Tell our mother I have come back with a wife. Tell Mother to make things ready for her."

The youngster said, "All right." He got his water and went home. "Oh, Mother, someone has arrived over there by the water. He comes with a wife who shines brightly, and he says he is my older brother."

The mother thought he was lying; she slapped him and told him to behave. The boy went back to the water and said, "Mother doubted me."

His sister-in-law told the boy, "Come here," and he did so. The child was small, with a pot belly. The wife brushed him: he became older and slimmer. He changed into a skinny little boy, more mature than before.

He went home again and told his mother, "Look what she did to me!"

His mother got madder still: "No!" she screamed and beat the boy again.

He went back to the water and said, "Oh, Mother beat me again. She said it was all make-believe, because my brother is long dead."

The man said, "No, this really is me. I walked away from here and traveled for a very long time, until I got to the home of Day, the father of my wife. He found me and told me where his house was." The sister-in-law took the boy and stroked him again, making him older and taller. His hair grew long and beautiful.

Again he went home. Again he was beaten. This is the fourth time now. Again he went back to his older brother. "Oh, my mother just beats me. She says you are just playing with me."

His sister-in-law took him again, brushed his hair and rubbed it with sweet oil. She brushed him and made him full-grown. He was a good, slender young man. She gave him fine clothes and said, "Go to your mother and have her look at what her new daughter-in-law has done for you." He went.

He looked so fine this time that his mother was completely taken in. She swept the house and cleaned it thoroughly. She scattered fresh feathery down everywhere {as is done to honor someone important}. She sprinkled water over the floor and the doorway. When she had everything done, she saw her son and his wife approaching.

The son came to the door and said, "Now do you recognize me? I am the one who walked away when my sister hurt my feelings."

They lived there. The wife really became pregnant. She gave birth to two babies, and they were stuck together. The twins grew up much faster than normal babies. Their father needed to make bows for them after only a few days.

There was an old lady named Bluejay, and she was a nosey know-it-all. She told everyone, "Oh, those little ones run around stuck together. They could be separated, and they would be two." Oh, she sneaks up on the little ones to separate them. She followed them and separated the little ones, and they died. The father had misfortune with his children, born stuck together and killed when separated.

The mother took it the hardest and blamed all of her in-laws for letting it happen. She took a sharp stick and stabbed everyone in the camp, releasing little monsters which flew away. {Thus all the blowflies came to be created.} Then she went to the place where she and her husband had come down and pulled on the rope left hanging there to carry messages to the earth above. The ladder was lowered, and the wife and husband went back to the sky world.

{That is the way things came to be. The Fly People were done in, and modern insects created. Although the wife left these bad creatures in this world, the couple also did some good. The husband brought down his treasures and the edible roots, like carrots. They left these for the good, hard-working people of today.}

That is all.

Basket Ogress

Told by Agnes James at Tulalip in 1952

A GROUP OF children knew a woman who lived all alone near the river. The children knew that she was lonely, and they wanted to go visit with her. When they asked their parents for permission to go, their parents said, "No. You can't go, because it is too far away: the Giant Woman might get you when you are away from home. The Giant Woman is powerful. She would put you in her huge clam basket."

The children ignored their parents. They got into a canoe and went on their way to visit the lonely woman. When night came, they made themselves a camp on the other side of the river. They built a fire and cooked their supper. One of the children was a hunchback. When the children divided their supper, Hunchback was given the tail part.

They traveled for several days. Each evening they would stop to camp overnight and eat their supper. Every time, they would give Hunchback the tail part for his share.

Hunchback finally said, "If you folks are always going to be giving me the tail part when I would really rather have the tips, I will call the Giant Woman!"

When night came again and they stopped to camp and eat their supper, it was still the tail part which he was given. Now Hunchback hollered! He hollered:

Come downhill, Giant Woman!
Come downhill, Giant Woman!
It is just the tail part
That I am given by my playmates.

The Giant Woman heard right away. "Oh, there is someone hollering at me!" She put her basket on her back and she walked. She was a huge person, this Giant Woman. She chewed on everything as she traveled.

She arrived where the children were. Right away she began to pick up the children one by one and put them into her basket. She grabbed Hunchback first and put him there. When all of the children were in the basket, the Giant Woman walked. She carried these children upland. Suddenly she could feel something catch at her basket. She thought, "Oh, it must be Hunchback who has caught onto something."

Hunchback had squirmed and squirmed until he managed to get himself up on top of the other children. Each time he came to a leaning tree he tried to grab ahold of it. No! He couldn't do it. On the fourth try, he did it.

Giant Woman went on walking. When she arrived at her home with the children she immediately gathered rocks and placed them on her fire to heat. When they were good and hot she began to take the children out of her basket. Then she found that Hunchback was missing. "Oh, Hunchback isn't here! Where is he? Maybe he managed to run away!"

Giant Woman ran!

Hunchback was in the canoe, shoving off from shore. He had a paddle with holes in it. This paddle had holes. When Giant Woman threw rocks at him, he held up his paddle and the rocks just went through. Hunchback paddled hard. Each time she threw a rock at him, he raised his paddle and the rock just went through a hole.

Giant Woman gave up. She went home and put more rocks on her fire. She wanted the rocks to be very hot to cook her supper fast.

The children huddled together and began talking to each other. They watched the Giant Woman heating all of those rocks on the fire.

Giant Woman noticed and said to them, "What are you children saying?"

The children carefully answered, "Oh, it is just that we are so happy for you that you are heating rocks. We would like for you to sing and dance before you cook us there!"

Giant Woman was so flattered at the request that she said, "All right!"

The children said, "You will dance!"

She proudly said, "Yes, I will." Now Giant Woman danced. She sang this as she danced:

The children will be roasted on the rocks!
The children will be roasted on the rocks!
The children will be roasted on the rocks!
The children will be roasted on the rocks!

The children said, "Oh my, but your song is so nice. Sing more!" And again Giant Woman sang and danced.

The oldest and strongest of the children were making plans: "We had better push her onto the hot rocks!"

Giant Woman asked, "What are you children saying?"

They cautiously answered, "Oh, we are just so happy for you!"

They whispered to each other, "When she comes near us, let's all push her!"

Oh! Giant Woman was coming closer, singing:

The children will be roasted on the rocks!
The children will be roasted on the rocks!
The children will be roasted on the rocks!
The children will be roasted on the rocks!

As she came close to them, all of the oldest, strongest children pushed her. Right onto the hot rocks she fell! She screamed, "Remove me, children! Remove me from the fire and I will return you to your home!"

One of the children said, "Get a forked stick, and we shall remove your grandmother from the fire. We shall remove her. Get a forked stick!"

However, the children took the forked stick, and everyone pressed her down onto the hot rocks until she was just stuck there, roasting!

That is the end of the story.

Coyote

Told by Andrew (Span) Joe in English
at Swinomish in 1954

THIS IS A syəhub, a story that really happened before the change. It is about Coyote and his daughter. There was a tribe that they belonged to. And there was a family from another village who got stuck on Coyote's daughter. They wanted a young child of theirs to marry this daughter. Old Coyote, he kind of acted like a big shot. There were lots of things that he wanted them to prove before his daughter married the young man. Coyote knew that his daughter was a good runner, like the fastest animals. Coyote said: "Tell you what I will do. If you beat my daughter running in a foot race, I'll let you be my son-in-law."

At first they brought a lot of stábigʷs (ceremonial gifts) to Coyote so that he might accept the suitor. Kind of like buying the girl. When the races were going to be on, this family brought all kinds of food to feed everyone witnessing the race. All of the people from neighboring villages and all of the different animals knew what was going to take place so they gathered. It made the family of the contestant important people because they collected all of this food. The valley was crowded with people, and birds and animals and even fish. They placed the judges, people who had been chosen because they were known to have syuid (the most powerful control power) so that there would be no crooked work.

The races began. At daybreak, Coyote and his daughter woke up. Coyote said: "This is the day that you are going to prove our superiority. The young man who beats you will have to come from a higher family."

The races went on. Coyote's daughter was up at daylight, well advised by her family. She easily beat her opponent. Coyote turned to the boy's family and said: "No hard feelings. Your son didn't beat my daughter and the races shall continue. Anyone who can beat my daughter will become her husband."

The next opponent was Raven. An argument started because Raven had wings. Coyote said: "This is a foot race on the ground. You will have to use your legs, not your wings."

Raven wondered what to do; he knew that he couldn't run very fast. He said: "I'll just use my wings and keep my feet on the ground. That will be legal." He kept up a little bit at first, but he got tired because his feet were not used to running a foot race. He was beaten, but he wasn't about to give up. He called for his cousins and all the other birds with wings who were his cousins. He called them to come and help him to entertain so that he could get another chance.

Coyote said: "No, my daughter has beaten you once and she would beat you again. It's no use."

Raven said to Coyote: "But if I feed all of the people, I'll get another chance, won't I?" This was part of his scheme. He was pretty schemey.

But Coyote was pretty tricky, too. He answered: "All right, I'll accept another race if you can't flap your wings."

Raven wilted. He had to go through with it, though, because he had asked his cousins to feed all of the people.

The races started again after Coyote's daughter had rested for a few days. Coyote's new regulations made it much tougher for Raven. Coyote's daughter walked off with the race. Raven gave up.

Mink, another schemey character. He wanted to race the girl. He was really aching to get the young woman. He was of that type that really has to have a woman. He was in heat all of the time. Every time he walks around, he wants everyone to see what he's got, what makes a man out of him. He was pretty well-to-do this way. When he saw this young lady, he thought: "Boy! I'm going to be the first one to get her." But he was too much of a little runt. His legs weren't long enough. However, he had a word in syuid that made his legs stretch, so that he could run and hop fast. He had another word in syuid that he used to slow down his opponent. He was such a man that he was bigger in that certain place than anyone else. Now it was time for the races to take place.

Coyote's daughter was up at daybreak as usual. Mink was not supposed to use syuid. It was crooked to do that. He got up before daylight and, he went out to the place where the race was going to take place, and he named everything on the ground. He tried to fix everything in syuid to control things in his favor. At first he managed to slow the girl down. About one quarter of the way, the judges knew what had happened. They punished Mink, and they called the names of his muscles, veins and tendons in the language of syuid, and Mink slowed down. The judges wanted the race to be honest. Mink slowed down and he lost the race. Now he argued that he wanted four chances. He knew that if he could slow the girl down one quarter of the way on the first chance, then he could slow her down one half of the way on the second chance, and on the third chance he could slow her down three-quarters of the way, and then on the fourth chance he could beat her.

Coyote was pretty clever himself. He said: "The first contestant only wanted two chances, and he was just as easily beaten the second time. That's all I'll give you is two chances."

Mink wilted as he thought, "What's the use?" His syuid didn't work.

Goat, way up in the mountains, knew what was going on all of the time down in the valley. He had his home in the caves of the highest mountain peaks. He was really siʔáb (upper class). Didn't have to be down in the valley to know what was going on. He just knew through his dreams. He really knew syuid. He was wealthy. That is why he lived on the very peaks of the mountains. About that time everybody was giving up on the girl. He knew that. He knew that nobody could outrun that girl, Coyote's daughter. She felt pretty confident after she had beaten everyone. She walked around free-like now. She was proud of it. She tried to challenge everybody now. She would take all comers, but she didn't take a liking to any of them. That made it easier to beat them. Goat, through his dream, heard all about this. He knew what was taking place without being there. One morning he woke up before daylight, and he started to talk to his son. His son was a very good listener. He said: "Yesterday you were a boy, but today you are a man. I'm going to take you to those people who are celebrating down in the valley. I think that girl is good enough for you, and I think you are going to bring her home."

Goat also had a daughter. Her mother was dead. The daughter's name was xʷələ́xʷələʔ. She was a mind reader. She wanted to go along. Her brother didn't want her along because she would be a nuisance among the people, reading everybody's mind and telling about it. His sister promised she would not do that, but she wanted her brother to understand that for anyone who made fun of the Goat family, she would come out with their thoughts. If she didn't go along, he wouldn't win. Goat was listening to the argument. He said: "Your sister is right. We will have to take her along. You will have to have company for the daughter of Coyote when you bring her back." So they took sister along. She was doing all right, doing what she promised. Every time she came close to someone who hated her brother, she would nearly make a slip. Her brother would warn her with a sign like a raised finger or something.

The Goats packed for their journey. They always had the valuable parts of the meat, the tallow, the fat which the people up there used for diapers for a child in the mountains. It dries and forms a little soft blanket of tallow. They had a big supply of dried meat, all kinds of wealth from the mountains, a whole houseful, just wrapped up. All three of them were powerful. With syuid they made this into a small package, so small that you could hardly see it. The boy packed the little package on his shoulder. They got directly down to the valley and they said: "We are coming to play. We are going to entertain all of the people who are gathered there. We don't care if we don't beat your daughter, but we are going to take her home."

Old Coyote looked down at the legs of Goat and he thought, "Gee, they look skinny! How is that young man going to beat my daughter with legs like that?" As these thoughts came to Coyote, xʷələ́xʷələʔ broke out for the first time. She laughed: "Yohohoho!" in a funny way, a kind of critical laugh to think that Coyote could think thoughts like that. Her brother shoved her and she shut up. Coyote told Goat: "No one can beat my daughter, but we'll set the races for tomorrow." xʷələ́xʷələʔ didn't sleep all night. She paced up and down the race course. She wanted to absorb all of the negative thoughts and feelings against her family. At daybreak she went to join her group just as they were getting up.

Goat said to his son: "We shall gain control of every one of those judges. We came to entertain and feed the people." When they opened up their little pack, it filled the room. There was plenty of food for weeks and weeks to feed all of the people, to make the people open their eyes and see what siʔáb is." When Goat said this, Coyote just wilted. He knew that there was something about Goat.

The races started. The judges were sitting at the finish line. The race started. xʷələ́xʷələʔ was walking back and forth. She didn't want to bother anybody. Son of Goat was just jumping along and he passed the girl like nothing.

Coyote said: "xʷúi??!" That meant he recognized defeat and his spiritual powers came right out. He turned to Goat and said: "You have beat me with your power. You have great powers. You are siʔáb and you shall have my daughter." Goat said: "We'll stay and feed the people." They entertained, and they all had a great time.

The time came for them to go home and take the girl with them. Coyote said: "I must go along with my daughter." He was full of mischief.

Son of Goat fixed his bride through syuid, so that she could climb the mountain. The next morning they got ready. It takes all day to climb those cliffs. The son of Goat didn't do anything for his father-in-law. They left the valley and came to the foot of the mountain, the very steepest of cliffs. Both families climbed together.

Coyote looked up at the cliff and he thought: "How am I going to climb that steep mountain?" xʷələ́xʷələʔ read his mind and broke out laughing: "How is he going to climb that steep mountain?"

Her brother shoved her and told her to keep quiet. Coyote's son-in-law said: "I thought you were great, you could go anywhere. You said that you were siʔáb and knew everything."

Then Coyote found out that he knew nothing about syuid. Son of Goat then named every part of Coyote's body and fixed him up. Coyote doubted it.

Then xʷələ́xʷələʔ broke out again: "How am I going to strengthen my body so that I can fix it up so that I can climb that mountain?"

Her brother shoved her and told her to stop that. Away they went.

Sure enough, Coyote was way up in the lead all of the time. It wasn't his power that was giving him strength, it was his son-in-law's syuid. *Sure, he, Coyote, is greater than anybody! Bigger than anybody else!*

When they were nearing the house of Goat, his son-in-law warned him. "Never get scared when my dog shakes himself. He shakes everything off from himself, and when he does this whole earth starts to quiver when a stranger comes near my home."

Coyote kind of half-way believed that his son-in-law had power. As soon as they got close to the home of Goat, this dog shook, brushing himself off. Boy! That mountain just quivered! Coyote had to hold on to the sides and he was so scared. xʷələ́xʷələʔ just laughed and voiced his thoughts: "There must be some big beast that has control of this mountain!" His son-in-law had warned him not to get scared. Coyote thought: "I guess that my son-in-law is great. He is a man that has been brought up right." xʷələ́xʷələʔ interpreted aloud.

They went into the home of the Goat family in the cave. There was everything you could think of in this big home. There was food of all kinds. Coyote was so happy. "I guess my daughter is going to be happy with this man." He was beginning to admit that these were great people.

Then a child was born to the daughter of Coyote and the son of Goat. It grew up fast. It had diapers made from the thin layers of tallow. Coyote wanted to be baby-sitting all of the time because of this tallow. Tallow was good food, and he was picking at it all of the time when he was changing the diapers. He wanted to change the diapers all of the time. He was getting schemier, worse and worse. He got stuck on an instrument made from a little gʷádaʔkʷ (horn) of a little elk or deer. It was a kind of awl, very sharp. He was going to take it and go home now. Coyote was going back to the way he had been in the valley. His daughter accused him of eating the tallow. His own daughter did that. He got to hating her. His son-in-law stuck up for him, but his daughter didn't want anyone to take what her child was using.

Coyote took the little horn awl one night, and he started to walk home with it, but everything in the house was controlled by syuid. You can't steal anything from the house of great people and get away with it. That was the power of this family—syuid. They were honest. He walked all night, walked and walked, and he thought he was going down the cliff. Finally he went to sleep. He thought that he was half-way home now. But it was the syuid, the power that made this home wealthy, that made him think that he was going down the cliffs. But all this time, he was just going around in the house.

When he woke up, his daughter said: "What are you trying to do, Dad? You are trying to steal your son-in-law's property."

It was a lie. His son-in-law told his wife: "Don't say anything to your father."

Coyote heard his good son-in-law defend him, but still he got worse. Now he was going to take the foods home with him. Not everything, but most of it. *He was bigger than anybody else because he now had a grandson from good blood!* But that was the way he always was when he was with people bigger than he. So, that night he took half of the food and the horn awl. He was going to take a lot while he was at it. So, he walked, and he called everything in the name of syuid to make his pack small. He was really traveling fast now so that he would be home by daylight. He just had to be there by daylight. He had everything, half of the stabigʷs of the Goat family. Their dried winter foods and things for feasts. He had the power now! He didn't know that it was the syuid of his son-in-law which really helped him. He was to be the big shot down in the valley. He was walking when he looked over and saw his daughter and his son-in-law just watching him. *He had just gone to sleep in this house!*

That was the turning point. They were through with him. His daughter said: "He'll never quit doing that. He'll keep doing that until he damages us in some way. He should be punished. He has turned back to what he was before we ever met you folks. I'll never leave you, though, because I have your child, and we are going to raise him. We must protect this child. How shall we punish my father?"

Her husband said: "I hate to punish anyone, but I guess you are right. He is your dad, and you know how he is. You are a mature-thinking person now, and you must protect your son and raise him to be siʔáb. For the sake of our child I will punish Coyote. He will have to get out the hard way by begging x̌áx̌ad (the supernatural one) to give him a gift so he can clear himself and get himself out of this prison that I am going to put him in." The young man said: "We are going to take everything out of this home. We will not leave anything."

The whole family packed everything. Then the son of Goat named the icy part of the mountain: "dxʷq̓áxʷigʷədìd"—"freeze it from the inside," in the language of syuid.

They froze the whole mountain where Coyote was. Now the son of Goat called for snow to come piling thicker and thicker to cover Coyote, then to melt and become ice. Coyote could see through the ice. He could see the sky and the stars and the sun. The ice was so thick he could not get out. The family had deserted him! They left the mountains, and that is why snow is on the mountains today. The hills have plenty of snow because of Coyote's punishment. Goat ordered that, and that showed how great they were. The snow gets thinner and thinner, and then it turns to rain as you come down from the mountains because they didn't want to punish all of the people.

Well, there he was in prison. He could see all around. The house became kind of round, and the snow became thicker and thicker, and then it melted a little bit and turned to ice. He could see through it. Then he began to beg xáxad and the adᶻʔúladəd (impurities) came out of him. He had no food. Coyote began to dream that xáxad was going to come and help him a little bit, with one condition. If he does wrong when he gets out of the ice house, he is going to be punished. He then followed xáxad's directions. He was told: "You shall rub your feet and toes so that the heat of your body wears and melts the snow and ice down." He did this with his feet and his toes, and they began to wear down. Then he used his knees and then his elbows, then his head, and they wore down. At last he used his tongue, and he made a little hole in the ice. He just couldn't sleep. He had to keep going to keep the hole open. He dozed for a few seconds, and xáxad said, "You shall take everything apart of your body. Unjoint everything, and put them through that little hole to get out. But you will have to use the words of syuid."

He started with his eyes. Then he started to worry: "What am I going to do without my eyes?" But this was what xáxad had told him to do. Next were his feet. He kept wondering why his eyes were to go first. This was where the punishment was going to take place. He unjointed his feet. It was hard without seeing. Then up to his knees, his hips, and then his ass. That is where the worst thing of all that comes out. He just hated it. He smelled it break wind when he passed it by his nose. He hated that smell. Then it was all right. Then he got his gut and his ribs and then his heart. It was pretty tough. "How am I going to protect it?" Then he begged again. He took off his fingers and then his shoulders. He had to name everything through syuid. xáxad was dishing it up for him because he didn't know the word until he unjointed the part. The words came from xáxad right then. Then he came to his throat. He had an awful time. He wondered how he was going to talk and name the names of his body.

xáxad told him: "That is why you are so greedy, always stealing and have plenty to eat. You are ʔəsq̓iyuq̓ʷ (greedy throat)." Then he was told what to say about throat. Then the cəqʷ (anus), that craves for food and is greedy. "That is the reason you are crooked. That is why you think you are better than anyone else!" After he got his throat through the hole, he went to his jaw and then his brains. Then he got out and he put himself together.

Then he heard a bird that was Raven flying about and having a good time. He was having a great time! Coyote had a feeling that something wasn't right. The *bird* was the punishment. Raven knew that this punishment was coming and that he was the one to do the punishing. But he was a crooked guy, too! He had a hunch through x̌áx̌ad not from his own mind. Coyote thought that he was going to get even with his in-laws, but this didn't turn out. He was punished again. Through x̌áx̌ad he was let out. The punishment came through that hole. After he got out and put himself together, he forgot the words for his parts because he had that crooked feeling. He wanted to put his eyes on first. But, no, that feeling caused him to start from his toes up. After he completed himself, the last thing was his eyes. That old Raven got away with them! It was going to be a punishment. He forgot all the wordings of those joints because he had had that evil feeling in him, which he had promised he wasn't going to do any more. When he discovered that his eyes were gone, he said: "That's why Raven was glad and was having a lot of fun when he saw my eyes. Maybe I have done wrong by thinking of getting even!" He wondered how he was going to find his eyes. x̌áx̌ad seemed to tell him: "You know that part that you hated in your body when you were taking yourself apart? There is still something in that bag that smells. You must take that part. There are two (turds). You call them your brothers."

He sat down and they talked to him. He had to ask them: "What am I going to do now, my younger brothers?" They said: "You go to that bush and talk to the leaves and name them and put them where your eyes were, and you'll see a little bit until they get dry."

He could see a little bit, and then he walked to the west. Then he came to another bush to get leaves because the other ones became dry. There were two girls there picking berries. They said: "What are you doing, Coyote? What are you doing?"

He said: "I'm picking these berries here, elderberries." But it wasn't the bush where those berries grow.

So the girls looked at him, and they saw that he did not have any eyes. "It seems that he doesn't have any eyes."

He said: "I can see a small white star way up there in the sky."

"It is daytime, and you couldn't see any star!"

"Yes, I *can* see a star! Come close!"

One of the girls, the youngest, said: "Don't go over there!" But the older girls aren't always cautious like their younger sisters, because they are treated like pets and are given nothing but scoldings all of the time when they grow big, but it soaks into the younger ones.

Coyote said: "You come close to my arm. You come close to my hand, and you can see right through it." The girl came near. "Put your head right against my arm." As soon as she got near, he dug her eyes out with his fingers, and he went right along.

The younger sister said: "I told you so! Just by not listening. You never listen to your parents!"

After he got the eyes, he could see pretty well. He connected them where his own eyes had been. Now he was going to look for his own eyes. So he walked and walked and walked. He said: "I will ask my younger brothers what to do now—what do I do now?" They said: "You walk along the beach for a while and come to a family." He said: "Go on back inside. I knew that all along." That is what he hated and where he was getting the advice. This was the punishment from x̌ax̌ad. He walked and walked, and he came to a strange noise—coughing. It was stúq̓ʷub. Sickness, like a cold, the cough that causes fever. It was an old lady. She was sick and she was living all alone in an old home. Coyote thought, "I have younger brothers who advise me." He asked them what to do.

They said: "This old lady has two grandchildren. They are out. The old lady will tell you where they are. You question this old lady about how her grandchildren act and dress and what she cooks for them, everything. How she acts when they come back from the celebration they have gone to." The old woman kept on coughing.

He said to his brothers: "I thought so." He really didn't know anything. He just thought he did, through his brothers' advice. He got all of that information from the old woman about her grandchildren, when they come and what they do. She told him everything. He planned to kill her now, and he would be stúq̓ʷub and be the grandmother of her grandchildren when they returned. That was the advice his brothers gave him. He was to imitate this old woman, Sickness. He told her: "I'm going to burn you up." He was just talking.

She said: "You do me good if you burn me. You just help me out!"

So he said: "I'll do that to you. I'll take advantage of you." He was going to kill her that way, through intercourse.

She said: "You'll help me out." She really wanted him to do that, and she was pleased. It was how she came on earth, through that stuff.

He said: "I'll get nettles and rub them all over you." She gave in right away. The nettles were what he used to kill her. That is the medicine, nettle roots, for a cold. Then he killed her with the nettles, and he got rid of her. He then put on her clothes, and he fixed himself every bit like she was, and he imitated her. But he didn't quite act like the old lady when the grandchildren were getting near.

When they came in he was pretending to be asleep. He never did that before. Then he started to cough and cough. The grandchildren said: "Guess grandmother is beginning to feel better today." But it was Coyote himself.

"How was it where you folks were today?"

The older one said: "A lot of people were having fun with Coyote's eyes, rolling them. They were betting which eye would win, and they were having a great time." The younger girl was suspicious that something was wrong with their grandmother, but not the older one. The advice hadn't sunk in, and she was kind of crazy-like.

Their grandmother who was really Coyote wanted to go to this celebration. He knew where he was going to find it. "I know I'm kind of bad off, but I want to see what they are celebrating before I die."

So they took him over. They packed the old lady, the younger one first. He was imitating the old lady perfectly, but not perfectly enough for the younger girl. She was first to pack Grandmother. They went just a little ways, and he became tempted and wiggled around and felt around her. She threw him down hard. The older girl got after her because she threw Grandmother right on the ground hard. The older one put him on her back. He kept working down. She knew what he was doing, but she paid no attention to it because she was kind of crazy, anyway. Finally, he felt around her private parts, and she let him down easy. She said to her sister: "I'm getting tired." But she kind of liked it. She was kind of crazy. So the youngest girl packed him, and then she threw him down hard. So the older girl packed him all the way to the place.

He said: "You bring me right to the goal where they are playing with Coyote's eyes, where the people are betting valuables." It seemed like when he sat there his eyes could understand him. The first thing he said; he spoke low: "Come near!" And while the eyes were rolling, they kind of shifted over to the old lady. The people kind of noticed. The second time they jumped over to her. The third time they nearly hit her face. And the fourth time he named in syuid: "You come, eyes, come to my face! You disappear into my head, where my eyes belong!"

Then he said: "You no-good-for-nothing people, my eyes you have control of!" Now he jumped out of those clothes of stúq̓ʷub, and he left them on the ground. That is why the cold today is not as strong as it used to be. He left.

The people chased him, and they were gaining on him when he thought of his brothers again. One of them said s "You throw me out and I'll turn into a river!" So he did, and it slowed up the people who were chasing him.

Then they crossed the river and were gaining on him. He asked the other brother. He was told: "You throw me across your track, and everything will turn into fog. You go out on that island by yourself, and they'll never find you." So when Coyote went to that island, they lost track of him.

That is the end of the story.

Mink and the Changer

Told by Martha LaMont at Tulalip in 1963

THERE WAS MINK. Mink was out traveling around when he came upon a very beautiful sight: a nice hot fire with salmon browning on skewers. The skewers were made of ironwood and leaned just the right distance from the heat. Oil from the salmon was beginning to drip, so Mink knew that this fish was just ready to eat. What a temptation! He was so hungry, and the old man was sound asleep there by the fire. Mink quickly took the cooked salmon off the skewers and ate it. It was so good, he ate all of it before he walked on.

He traveled down by the salt water, then upland along the hills, then back down to the water's edge. He developed a great thirst as he traveled, and he stopped for a drink of water every chance he had. Finally he got to a river where he found lots of salmon. He took the fresh salmon out of the river, and he fixed it and put it near the fire. The salmon would cook slowly while he went out exploring. Mink was all alone. His younger brother was not with him. After a while Mink got sleepy and decided to lie down and take a little nap.

He did not know that the Changer was walking around now. The Changer was walking along the water's edge, finding people and questioning them. He was curious about the welfare of the people.

As the Changer walked, he came upon Mink, who was asleep. The Changer thought, "Isn't this good salmon that Mink is roasting here!" He knew the kind of person that Mink was. The Changer was hungry now, so he thought, "Maybe I had better just help myself to this salmon that Mink has cooked here." So he did. He took the cooked salmon and ate until he was satisfied;

then he walked on. He traveled, going along the edge of the salt water and then on up into the hills and back down to the water.

Mink finally woke up. As soon as he saw that his cooked salmon was gone, he knew! The Changer had taken it! He was rather a shrewd fellow also, kind of supernatural. He knew that the Changer was traveling around. He had heard about him. Mink thought, "He is the one who stole my salmon!"

Mink ran upland, and he could see the Changer walking there ahead of him. "Yes, indeed, it was the Changer who ate my salmon," Mink thought angrily. His empty stomach rumbled. Now he quickened his pace and ran upland, above and ahead of the Changer. When he was slightly ahead, he stopped and made a little water. *He made a little water that spilled downhill!* He knew that the Changer would be getting thirsty because he had eaten all of the salmon. Mink continued on upland, ahead of the Changer. When he got ahead of him a bit more, again he made a little water. It spilled downhill. It seemed to be just a little stream of water spilling downhill.

Then Mink said to the Changer, he said to him (because *that one* had become thirsty, and he had put his face down into the little stream of water that he had just happened to see spilling downhill, and he had taken a big drink the Changer had taken a big drink!—), Mink said to him: "Yeah, yeah, someone drank some young fellow's pee!"

"Oh, the dirty thing! Yuck! Mink must have tricked me!" But the Changer let this incident pass. He just spit and walked on. After he had walked quite a distance, again he saw a little water spilling downhill—a nice little stream of water, and he was so thirsty. His throat was really parched!

Again Mink taunted him: "Yeah, yeah, he drank some young fellow's pee!"

"Oh, the dirty thing! It's that Mink mocking me again!"

Mink was following the Changer and making fun of him. He felt he *had* to get the best of the Changer, since the Changer had stolen and eaten his salmon.

The Changer stopped now and looked at Mink. He spoke in a voice like thunder: "You, mink! Because you have behaved like this, treating me with disrespect and making fun of me, I decree that from now on you shall be nothing but a mink, an animal running about on old tree snags and traveling in and on the water and upland around old dead logs!"

He took Mink and threw him down to the water. Mink swam. He was changed into the animal he is today.

This is where you catch a glimpse of him now and then: among the old tree snags near the water. There Mink will be!

That is the end.

Pheasant, Raven, and the Hunters

Told by Martha LaMont at Tulalip in 1964

PHEASANT AND RAVEN lived there. They lived next door to each other, this Pheasant and Raven. Pheasant had many children. I don't know who Pheasant's wife was, he just had a wife. Raven also had many children, and qʷə́lqʷəlič was his wife. They lived there.

Pheasant went for a walk. He said to his wife, "I am going to walk up toward the mountains, I am just going for a walk without any special destination in mind. I am going out for a walk, and I am going toward the mountains." So Pheasant went. He wandered aimlessly. He just wandered. He and his family were hungry; they didn't have enough food, it seemed.

As he walked, he came upon two young men sitting down. They have two dogs. The dogs bark and growl at him as he walks along. They snap and bite at him. The two young men say to him, "Call your dogs, Pheasant, call them."

Pheasant replied, "No, no, honorable sirs, I won't call them. They are not my dogs. Maybe they belong to you. I don't have dogs, I am poor."

The owners of the dogs called them, and the dogs sat down; they lay down.

Pheasant went and joined the young men. They asked him, "Where do you come from, Pheasant?"

Pheasant answered, "Oh, I am just wandering around. I was walking upland toward the mountains, but over that way is where I live. I am just wandering around. My children are very hungry."

The hunters replied, "Oh!" Then they said to him, "And is that your deer lying there on the other side of you, that elk which is wrapped up, lying there? There is an elk on the other side of you all wrapped up and ready. It is already packaged up, that elk!"

Pheasant replied, "No, honorable sirs. It is not mine. I do not have any game. I am poor. Maybe that food belongs to you folks; it is your large animal."

They liked his honesty. They said to him, "Pheasant, you will sit there. We are going to butcher the elk, We are going to wrap it up for you to take home. We are giving it to you."

Pheasant said, "Oh, honorable sirs, you will indeed be saving the lives of my children! My children are always hungry. They and my wife are so unfortunate. We are living in poverty."

The hunters then prepared and wrapped the elk. They made it into a small package and they gave it to Pheasant to pack. They fixed young cedar limbs and braided them into rope which they used for tying the bundle. They tied it into a small, compact bundle, this large elk which they gave to Pheasant. This was real food which he was given. Then the hunters said to him, "You go ahead and heft this bundle, Pheasant. You are going to pack this now. We are making it light! We are going to make it light so that it will not be heavy for you to carry."

Pheasant gratefully acknowledged their gift, and he said, "You folks will really be helping me with your generosity!" He sat down while the hunters put the pack on his back.

Then they instructed him. "Now you will stand up, Pheasant, and you will walk." They helped Pheasant to his feet, and as he went, the hunters gave him parting instructions. They said, "We trust that you will manage to pack this load which we have lightened for you. However, if you stop to rest, do not turn around and look at your pack. You just go on downhill. Do not turn around to look at it! You just keep walking until you arrive at your home. Then you may look at it and unwrap it. It will be your food to eat. There is a lot. It is a very large elk which we have given to you."

Pheasant now thanked the hunters. Then the poor thing who had been given this food went on. He walked on until he felt the need to rest. When he stopped, he lifted the weight of his pack off his back by leaning against a log with the bottom of his pack resting up on the log. He remembered that the hunters had told him not to turn around and look at his pack, so he just kept his face and eyes looking forward. Each time he stopped to rest, he did the same thing and said to himself, "I will not turn around and look at my pack, because I was told not to." He walked on until he arrived home with this bundle of food which he had been given.

He said to his wife, "We will unwrap this gift from the hunters. I found the hunters up in the mountains, and they gave me this food. Such good fortune they have brought us!" So Pheasant and his wife unwrapped the pack and they spread it around. The hunters had it all fixed up, all cut up. They were indeed hunters, as they had appeared to be. He had not just imagined their presence.

He gave his children the tallow which the hunters had included in the bundle. The little pheasants went outside, and they ate there as they played.

Raven saw them right away, and he said, "Hey! What is that white food that is being eaten by the children of Pheasant?" He went. Raven rounded up his children and told them, "You go on and look at what the Pheasant children are eating. Go on and look at it, see what it is they are eating."

So his children went. They stealthily moved closer with their wings fluttering close to the ground as they crept nearer.

The little pheasants just became annoyed and angry at them and told them, "Get away, you are getting dust all over us, you little Ravens."

They found out anyway. They found out what the pheasant children were eating. Pheasant's children were so mad at them! The little Ravens just went inside, where they told their father, "Oh, the children of Pheasant are feasting on tallow!"

When Raven heard this he wondered, "Where did they get that?" Raven went right over and asked Pheasant, "Where did you get your food?"

Pheasant courteously replied, "Oh, sir, I found some good, kind hunters, and they are the ones from whom we got this food. They gave me this large bundle to pack away as a gift from them." Pheasant gave Raven some cooked food for his wife.

Raven made just a few mouthfuls of this food; he gulped it down. He didn't share any of it with his wife and children. He finished every morsel of it himself. Then he said, "Why couldn't it be me, cənəx̌imáligʷəd, who could also find the hunters? Then he informed his wife: "I am going to travel."

Then he traveled. He climbed.

Pheasant was happy to give food to his friends and relatives; they gladly ate what they were given. Everyone was pleased. They all ate for a long time, because there was a lot. There was lots of meat from this big elk.

Raven went, and he arrived and found the hunters at the very same place where Pheasant had found them. The dogs barked at him. Raven's presence was made known by the barking dogs.

"Aha!" the hunters exclaim to each other. They tell Raven, "Call your dogs, Raven, call them, call them."

So Raven calls, "təməlíš, təməlíš, təməlíš." No. The dogs just keep growling, and they snap and bite at him. He calls the dogs "təməlíš," pretending to own them. He doesn't say, as Pheasant had, "They are not mine."

Raven, of course, is a cheat and a liar!

The hunters called off the dogs. Then they asked Raven, "Is that your game, Raven?"

Raven answered, "Yes, it is mine. I am a hunter. I am a hunter, that is why I was able to kill that game."

The hunters then said, "Go ahead, then, Raven, and butcher your game."

Raven tried to take the meat, and he thought he was unwrapping it in order to butcher it. He couldn't do it.

The hunters pushed him away now, and they said, "Get away, Raven." They *know* him. They disdain him. The only noteworthy thing about him is the reputation he has because of the big rectum he has gotten from eating more than his share of food. They push him away. "Get away!"

Now they butcher this which they are giving to him. "Yes. We are going to butcher this for you." They spread the sliced, butchered meat around.

Raven gobbled down the tallow as it was cut. There was lots of tallow. As fast as the hunters put it down, Raven ate it, he ate it, he ate it. He ate it as fast as it was butchered and put down by the hunters who were butchering the game for him.

So. Then the hunters fixed it for him. When it was ready the hunters said to Raven, "You will pack this which we have given to you. You will pack it so that you may take it home to your wife and children."

"I was the hunter who killed this game," Raven proclaimed! So he packed this food which he had been given. He just went a little way before he stopped to rest. He said to himself, *"Why should I have to pack game when I myself am the hunter? Who says I am not to turn around and look at it?"* What he has in mind, though, naturally, is that he wishes to eat it! He turns around to look at his pack.

Instantly, the elk, which had been wrapped in a package for him to pack, became unwrapped. It ran, returned. It ran! In its place, however, now is just rotten wood. Rotten wood replaces the meat which had been wrapped for him before. He is now packing rotten wood, and he thinks it is the meat which he had been given. However, indeed, this elk had run away. It returned.

Now the hunters said about Raven, "Oh. It seems that Raven, as could be expected, turned around to look at the food which we gave to him. Here comes the elk arriving here. Raven must have disobeyed our command and turned around. I suppose he tried to eat it!"

It seems he had tried it. Now it was just rotten wood when he arrived home. His wife informed him that he just had a worthless bundle wrapped up: "This is just rotten wood wrapped up lying here. There is no meat or anything in this bundle."

Raven shouted, "What kind of stupid female nonsense are you spouting!" Now he vomited up the rotten wood which he had been eating. Raven actually got embarrassed about this, as he vomited up the evidence.

Still, he turned to his children and said, "Pheasant still has lots of food to eat. Why don't you go over and pick a fight with his children? Go on over and fight with the children of Pheasant. They are always eating tallow. Pick a fight with them." He told his children, "You will use these little fish from the creeks for your ammunition to throw at Pheasant's children."

So the children went and threw the little fish, and they hit Pheasant's children with these fish. Raven placed himself behind his children as kind of a catcher. As soon as he caught it, he ate it. As soon as he got it, he ate it, this stuff that was thrown at his children. This had been his plan. He had had this in mind when he urged his children to pick a fight with the Pheasant children.

Then they got mad at him because of what he was doing. As usual, Raven was just gobbling up the playthings of the children. Now the game was stopped.

His children were throwing the little fish from the creeks. The Pheasant children got mad at the little Ravens and said, "Go away, you folks, you get dust all over us!" The children of Pheasant find Raven's children offensive.

So that was the end of that. That was why he was so overwrought. What could he do to get food away from his friends?

That was the end of the story about Pheasant and Raven.

Coyote's Son Had Two Wives

Told by Martha LaMont at Tulalip in 1963

COYOTE AND HIS son lived in this village. Coyote's son's wives were Pigeon and Sawbill. Now Sawbill was a beautiful woman, white and lovely to look at, but Pigeon was dull and gray. She was not very good-looking, yet she was his son's wife, his daughter-in-law. They all lived there together with his son.

Old Coyote coveted his beautiful daughter-in-law Sawbill. He was tormented, wondering how he could manage to get her for himself.

He went out for a walk to relieve himself. He had to find a way to have that woman. Then he heard a voice! He was being spoken to by someone over there. This voice talked to him whenever he went to sit a while. When he got done, he would sit there and ask: "Oh, my little brothers, what can I do about this?"

His advisors knew him very well; they said, "If we help you, you will just say as usual, 'I knew all the time what to do!' Why don't you just fix that son of yours? Fix him with a spell that will cause him to get so confused that he will get lost and die far away some place. After that, you can get his wives!"

Coyote twisted his mouth and said, "Oh yes, that reminds me. I shall do that!"

He returned home to find that his son was back from hunting. Coyote was impatient to get things started. Suddenly he said to his son, "Over there! Isn't that the special bird you get feathers for your hunting arrows from? It had red on its wing. It's the bird that goes around the trees, the one that is called Sapsucker, I think."

"Yes, it's the one that has the feathers I'm out of. I'll go after it."

Innocently he went. He never suspected that his father had instructed the bird:

"As my son climbs after you, just lead him on.
Let him get near you before you go higher.
When my son gets to the top of the tree,
There will be a heavy fog,
And he will get lost!
This is what I have in mind."

The little bird followed instructions.

Now Coyote turned and said to his son, "What you hunt is climbing over there, my son. You should take off the clothes you have on and lay them over there. You could climb better without them."

As his son climbed higher and higher, Coyote stood below and helped. He pointed out each time when the bird was just out of his son's reach.

Just happening to glance down, Coyote's son saw his father winking up at the bird. He said, "Oh, why are you winking at this bird that I am hunting? So there is something *you* are doing that causes it to keep ahead of me!"

Coyote replied, "No, I am just fixing my eye, my son, I am just fixing my eye."

His son continued climbing after the bird. It kept ahead of him as it had been told to do.

When he could see that his son was high enough, Coyote waved *it*, the thing through which he urinates, and he created a heavy fog! His son got lost way up high there.

He went to the other side, his son did. He was immediately placed in a different world. He walked on, realizing that it was a different place. After a while he came upon an elder, who said to him, "Oh, my grandson, oh! Where do you walk from, my grandson?"

He replied, "Oh, grandmother, I am lost! Coyote, my father, caused me to walk and get lost here. He did this to me. Can you tell me how I can manage to get down to the place that I come from?"

"Oh, my grandson, there is that one who stretches things. He is called Spider. Old Spider over there. He is an old person, Spider, your grandfather. You will go to him and say, 'You haven't returned me below.'"

Coyote's son went then, and when he came to the old one, he took him by the hand and said, "I have come to see you, grandfather."

"Oh, my grandson," Spider quietly said to him.

"My father, Coyote, put a spell on me, causing me to get lost up here. I want to go home, and that is why I have come to you, my grandfather. Would you lower me down?"

The old one turned and said, "Oh, my grandson, what do you say to me that I should do this for you?"

"I would pay you."

"No, my grandson. There is no need to pay for correcting a wrong that has been done by your father. It is best that I should return you. There is a hole over there that I go through. We need to act fast, though, because when the hole is opened there is a strong wind that blows through, and the people up here notice it. I have a rope that will reach all the way down."

{The storyteller explains carefully here about the rope, in case the listener doesn't yet realize that this is a spider web. She explains that he takes it from himself and stretches it out, this thing that you find stretched on trees and bushes. Everything like flies and mosquitoes gets tied up in it— ugly, ugly!}

Grandfather Spider lowered Coyote's son back to earth.

Of course, Coyote had taken his son's wives, and he was married now. He had loudly mourned when his son got lost. He had cried: "Oh, my father, my father! Maybe my father has grown old, my father my father. My father has grown old, maybe!" He had pretended then that he had no father. He pretended that it was his father, Coyote, who had died. *But it was Coyote himself saying this!*

Coyote went home to the women who had been his son's wives. Pigeon *knew* him. "Oh, it is that bad old man who is saying that." She wisely kept her thoughts to herself.

When Coyote went to Sawbill, he turned to Pigeon and said, "I will not come to you in the beginning. Sawbill is the one I will be with first, because your father-in-law favored you."

Unsuspecting Sawbill just married her father-in-law!

They began walking. Pigeon walked along behind, crying. When evening came and they set up camp, Pigeon was told to stay far away from the newlyweds. "Don't come. You just stay far away where you are. Don't come near us." They chased her away. She remained where she was told, very sad.

They walked on. Suddenly, someone stepped on the tumpline which she had belted on. Its ends were dragging behind, and it was stepped on. Pigeon said, "What is the matter, what is happening to my belt?" She walked a little further on, and again her belt seemed to catch on something and pulled her. She turned around.

It is the one who had been her husband. There he is!

When Grandfather Spider's rope had returned him to his own land, Coyote's son had looked for his family. He had tracked the trail that his father and his wives had made.

Pigeon then saw the one who had been her husband, and she exclaimed, "Oh! It *is* you!" Pigeon is usually crying, because she had really liked her husband.

Walking way ahead, though, were Sawbill and her father-in-law, to whom she was now married. She thought he was her husband, the son of Coyote.

Pigeon said to her husband, "The newlyweds chase me away. They don't want me near them. My camp is to be far away from theirs. And why not just let it be that way, they're married now."

When Pigeon and her husband camped, he told her, "I want you to go ahead and keep going to them. If they insist that you leave, you will just keep going to them." Pigeon did as she was told, while her husband remained out of sight.

Pigeon went ahead and got close to them before she was told, "Don't you come, Pigeon. No! Stay over there, far away from us. Get away!" But no! Pigeon just kept on. She reached them and just stood there.

Coyote got up. Just as he stood up, his son appeared and stood there also!

Immediately, Coyote ran to his son. He held out his hands full of his son's clothes and said, "Here are your things, your armbands, your leg ties, your leggings—all your things!"

The son replied, "Why are you removing *your* clothes? Just leave them on, you seem to own them! They are your clothes, why should you remove them?

They walked. He said, "You and Sawbill just go on ahead. Let her now belong to you. She is not to return to me." Coyote walked on with his wife, Sawbill. Naturally, Pigeon and her husband went on together.

Now a river was made for them by this one, Pigeon's husband. Coyote and his wife crossed it. Good! He habitually swam, so he could cross it. They landed and again they walked. Soon they came to a bigger river that had been made for them. Again they crossed it all right and landed on the other side. Then a yet bigger river was made for them, big enough so they would drift away. Then they started to cross, and Coyote just drifted downstream. Away he went. Then Sawbill went. Sawbill, who could swim so well, just drifted away, but she managed to land on the other side of the river. The river was too big for Coyote to cross. He just drifted wherever the current carried him.

Luckily, he was pulled into the fishing weir put up by Snipe and Magpie. His clothing caught there and held him. He recognized that the weir belonged to these two women. They were good hunters. He immediately turned himself into a wooden platter, a very nice little container.

When Magpie and Snipe came down to check their weir, they saw this good platter, and Magpie exclaimed, "Look, here is a wooden dish that must have drifted down here and landed."

Her friend said, "It is a good wooden platter. Take it, my dear, take it. We are always short of serving dishes. It would be very nice to serve our cooked food on."

They took the platter home, where they built their fire. When their food was cooked, they were happy to have such a nice serving platter to put it on, instead of having to use just leaves on the ground. They ate their fill. They were glad to see that there were a lot of leftovers there on their new platter!

Then they went out to dig for other special food that they used. When they returned home, they thought they would eat the salmon they had left on their new platter. They said to each other, "We won't have to cook. We can just eat that good food we left." But no! There was not a crumb there.

"For goodness sake, my dear. The food we had roasted is all gone. There is nothing left on this wooden dish!"

This happened several more times before one of them decided she had had enough of it. The wooden platter was taken outside. "What is this wooden platter that I have been putting our food on? What I put there is eaten, and now we are hungry!" The angry one bashed it against a sharp rock, and it broke into many pieces.

As soon as it cracked apart, they heard: "S-oo-wah, wah ah. I shall be your little brother, s-oo-wah!" The crying came from a little baby all wrapped up and lying there. *Now he is a small child, wrapped up!*

"For goodness sake, my dear, pick up your little brother. We really ought to keep him with us!"

One of them felt a little suspicious, yet she couldn't turn her back on a little baby. A cradle was made for him and he was secured there. *This one who had been a platter was now a small child! Here it is Coyote himself who is doing this!*

The women proudly gaze at the child cradled in the cradle board, which leans against a big cedar tree. The baby coos as it watches the tree limbs wave above it. It contentedly sucks on the salmon fin they gave him when they left to hunt for more food.

As soon as the women leave, Coyote unwraps himself and cooks and eats. Then he gets back into the cradle and wraps himself the way the women had left him wrapped. He will be innocently cooing and gurgling when they return.

"Look at your little brother, he is growing so big and strong now," one of the women said.

The other one replied, "Our food is gone again! There is nothing left. What could have eaten it? What?" She turned to the baby: "Yes, look at this little brother, look at him!"

When they went out hunting one more time and returned to find their food was gone, they finally allowed themselves to realize the truth: "It is *that one* who has been stealing our food!"

{The storyteller didn't tell us what the women did to the scoundrel at this point. She leaves us to think up some way to punish Coyote.

She says, "That one was not a very long story!"}

The Seal-Hunting Brothers

Told by Martha LaMont at Tulalip in 1966

THESE WERE THE people who lived there: a man and his wife, his grandfather, and her two young brothers, who were hunters.

These brothers were great hunters on land and on the water. When they hunted out on the salt water, they used a canoe that they themselves had made. This canoe went skimming along with very little effort on their part when they hunted seal and porpoise.

The brother-in-law of the hunters arrived, and he asked his wife, their sister, "How are you, how have you been? Do your brothers give you any of the game that they get?"

She answered, "No, sir, no! They don't give us anything. Your children are as you see them here." The woman had two children. *She has, however, been given food.* Her brothers give her food that they have already cooked for her. They give her enough cooked seal, porpoise and fish to feed all of her family. They expect her to set some aside for her husband to eat when he returns from his work. The woman is always so happy to receive this food from her brothers, who are such good hunters.

Again her husband asks, "How are things, do they give you any food?"
Again the woman answers, "No!"

Her brothers have given her lots of food that they have already cooked for her and her family. They generously give food to everyone in this village by the salt water.

Each time her brothers bring food for their sister and her family, she and her children eat all of it. She never sets aside anything for her husband. She has her children sprinkle ashes from the fire on their wooden

70

platters, and then she rubs their mouths with the ashes to hide any traces of grease from the food that they have eaten.

When their father arrives home, he can see that they seem to be very hungry. Their mother has instructed them to be very quiet and to pretend to be hungry. They do as their mother tells them.

Now the woman's husband gets very angry as he thinks about his hungry family, and he asks his wife, "Your brothers as usual have not given you any food?"

His wife answers, "No, sir, no. They give us nothing! I understand that they do come in with lots of game. I just keep quiet. They never say to us, 'Here is some for you.' No! Just look at your children, they are so hungry. They have had nothing to fill their stomachs. They have had nothing to eat! The same is true for myself!"

However, she is full of food, this bad woman! {The husband of the story-teller adds—"White woman!"}

Now the man became very angry, and he talked to his brothers. He said, "We shall kill our brothers-in-law. What do you think about our killing them because they haven't given their sister any of their game?"

His brothers replied, "Just restrain yourself."

But their grandfather said, "We shall just put a spell on them, we shall just put a spell on them! You will pretend to see something way over on the other side of the harbor, and you will come and say to them, 'By the way, my brothers-in-law, isn't that what you usually hunt, bending itself back and forth on top of that rock way over there? There is a great big seal way over there. That is what you usually hunt. You could sneak up on it, if you went out in your canoe, you are such good hunters!'"

The woman's husband went to his brothers-in-law and spoke to them as the old man had told him to.

The hunting brothers replied, "You don't have to say any more, we're going!" They lifted up their canoe and took it down to the water before they brought their hunting gear and paddles down to put into it. Their canoe was very light, because it was their great hunting canoe.

They got into the canoe and went. As they neared the big rock, they could see that there was indeed a great big seal there, bending backward and making noises as seals usually do.

However, it was the work of the bad old man. He made the seal and instructed it to act just as if it were alive, and it was to swim away with the hunters. The world would be covered with a thick fog, and the seal was instructed to take the hunters somewhere across the ocean to the very edge. The world would be calm but covered with fog.

The young men went and harpooned the seal. It just arched itself there as a seal would do if it were hurt. Then it threw itself around. They were thrown around as they tried to overcome it. There they were on board their canoe. They were holding on. One of them was just steering the canoe with his paddle in the water as they went. The other brother had hold of the line to his harpoon, which was in the seal. After they had gone quite a way he opened his hand to let go of the line. *But he couldn't let go!* His hand was stuck! He was trying to let go because he knew that this bad animal would take them far away. No!

He realized that it was something unnatural, and he turned to his brother and said, "Maybe we have had a spell put on us by our brother-in-law's grandfather. Maybe that is why this has happened to my hand. I can-not seem to let go of the line attached to my harpoon! Just steer our canoe with your paddle and let this seal take us wherever he will." The brothers were pulled along in their canoe.

The earth was covered with fog instantly, as the seal swam away with them. Every now and then the seal would dive and surface. It did this for many days. It was night when the seal arrived with them at a certain place. There was land nearby. It had things growing on it. They could see this as the fog lifted and things became visible in the daylight. They had been released!

There floating in front of them was a great big cedar. {The storyteller's husband is chuckling at this point.} This cedar floating in front of them is covered with tangled roots and branches.

The brothers looked at each other and asked, "Where in the world is that thing that ran off with us? Where is it?"

The younger brother said, "Pull the line that is attached to your harpoon that was in the seal, and you will find out." The older brother began pulling at his line, and it took him right to the big branchy floating cedar. When he reached it he removed his harpoon. So it had been this log which he had speared, and that had been the thing which ran off with them when they

came under the spell! "That evil old man put a spell on us, and that is why we are far away," they thought to themselves.

"We are indeed far away," the younger brother said. "It seems that we have been taken clear across the ocean. We had better lift up our canoe and hide it behind those logs. Let's lie down behind it and be quiet. We might be seen by people who live here." The older brother agreed: "All right, let's do it!" They beached their canoe and then carried it to the other side of the driftwood. Then they lay down on the landward side of it and hid themselves.

There they were hiding when they saw a child come into view in a large canoe, the kind that is built to hold a whole family. The child came paddling this big canoe. They stole a look at him as he came and stopped there offshore. This child stopped. *This person that seemed to them to be a child stopped.* It was a male child. He was there for a long time, and suddenly he began to go to and fro from one end of the canoe to the other. Then he got down and he dove. They saw this child dive. He was there at the bottom of the ocean for some time. Suddenly he surfaced, and he was holding several halibut.

He put two of them on board. He had four. It seems that this is what he is hunting, halibut. Again the child dove, emerging again with four halibut, which he put into the canoe. The brother's mouths were watering as they saw the good food that this creature was getting. {The storyteller's husband chuckles here.}

The younger brother said, "This is what makes me hungry. What can we do about it? We could hurry and carry our canoe down and be there while he is diving and help ourselves to his halibut. Then we could get back to shore before he comes up from his dive."

The older brother agreed: "All right!"

They quickly carried their canoe down to the water and went out, took the halibut, put it into their canoe and paddled back to shore. They had been ashore there on the landward side of the driftwood for a long time with the halibut before the child emerged. He got into his canoe and he missed the food which he had caught. Then this is what he did—he pointed toward the shore. His hand was moving and suddenly it stopped and pointed to where they were. It stopped right there.

"What is he doing?"

"He was pointing around, and now he had stopped where we are." *They still think it is a child.*

However, this person is what people call a dwarf, an old one.

The child probably thought to himself, "I had better take these strange people who come from somewhere. And I shall also take their canoe." So he took both of them and put them on board his canoe; then he went after their canoe, put it in the water and tied it to his canoe. Then he got on board. There they were where he had thrown them in the middle of his canoe. He had kidnapped them! They were wondering where they would be taken.

He took them over the water around the point. The people who lived there were not the usual kind of people. Everything there was colored. Some houses were colored red, some white, some striped—but all were colored. There were lots of people living there. That is where the brothers were landed.

Before they arrived at their destination they were told, "Don't be afraid. One of our children will come for you." The brothers understood what was said to them. Now they knew that dwarves had kidnapped them. *They are grown adults, yet they are small like children.* There were lots of the dwarves walking around all over—little tiny people, yet they are grown-ups, adults.

The dentalia were piled high. This was their food. It was a shellfish which they could get when the tide was out. They also dove underwater to get this mollusk. They ate what was inside the shells. There were some very large ones.

These shells were things which the brothers prized. One of them exclaimed wistfully, "Gosh, just look at how many dentalium shells they have just there behind them. We should try to sort out some of the larger ones to take with us if we can manage to be taken home!"

As the child escorted them along, he said to them, "You mustn't be afraid. The people are just going to feed you; then they will want to hear where you are from." The child took them up from the shore to a place where there were longhouses clustered together. He took them inside and seated them there where their beds would be.

They could hear an old man talking on and on. They couldn't under-stand what he was saying. He was telling his people: "Look at these people. They are really people, wherever it is that they come from. Get busy and prepare some food. You women, be quick about preparing them something to eat! It should just be some soup, because they are very weak now and their stomachs aren't very strong." So that was what was prepared for them to eat, some salmon soup.

There were lots of salmon there of all kinds—king, silver, dog. All the salmon were there! There were also lots of ducks. There was a constant movement of ducks there toward the water.

The brothers ate lightly and finished. They had been without food for so long! After they had finished eating they were questioned about their own homeland. There seemed to be a woman there who could act as interpreter.

As their captors listened, the brothers carefully explained what had happened to them: "Our brother-in-law caused us all of our misfortune. He put a spell on us which caused my hand to stick to the harpoon line, and we were pulled here where you found us. Then that seal-like thing our brother-in-law fixed for us turned into a huge, branchy cedar tree, which surfaced and floated. We removed out harpoon from it; then we landed and hid. Later, we stole the catch of a person we thought was a child. He was diving right below us and throwing the halibut he was catching into his canoe. We were dying of hunger! We had been out in the fog for a long, long time while the spell was upon us. We have no idea where we have been taken."

They were told then: "This is the land of the dwarves where you have come. The people here are all dwarves. We can communicate with those salmon and those ducks of all kinds. Our language is the same!"

Now the brothers understood. They looked longingly at the ducks. They enjoyed eating duck.

Meanwhile, the grandmother of the two young men mourned. She mourned the loss of the two hunters. She could see a seal emerge as she cried out her sorrow in the song she sang there by the water's edge:

That is the game that you hunt
Emerging from the water, my child.
That is the game that you hunt
Emerging from the water, my child.
That is the game that you hunt
Emerging from the water, my child.

Indeed, the animals the brothers used to hunt are surfacing out in the water. Seal and other animals are emerging there a little way offshore. The grandmother knew in her heart that her children were lost, that someone had run off with them. She knew that a spell had been put upon them!

Now the dwarves and the ducks raided and fought each other. These ducks of all kinds came in on them from up above. They killed the dwarves. They just seemed to use the quills from their feathers. As the feathers came out, the ducks shot them at the dwarves, and the dwarves died then and there. They died right then and there! The quills of the feathers stuck, and they died. The brothers just watched as the dwarves lay all over the place, dead!

Then these ducks came swarming inside, creating a great noise as they flew. One brother said to the other, "Hey, we could get ourselves a few if we were to hit them with our paddle. We could have ourselves a good duck feed. There are lots of good ducks coming right in here!" He went into action and chased the ducks, hitting at them with a paddle. The other brother followed behind picking up all the ducks that had been hit and killed. When they had gotten enough, they took away the dead ones.

They could hear one diving duck calling out to the rest, "Raise your arms, my brothers. Those are human beings who are doing you in! Raise your arms, my brothers. Those are human beings who are doing you in!" Oh, how the ducks raised their arms, making a great sound as they flew out and away in fright! These are human beings knocking them down!

The brothers only hit them because they wanted food to eat.

They looked at the dwarves. What had caused them to die, what could it have been? They looked at them carefully. These dwarves just seemed to be stuck with shafts from the duck feathers. {The storyteller's husband chuckles at this point.} The brothers pulled a few of the feathers out. The dwarves regained consciousness and got up! The brothers gave life back to all the dwarves.

The people now said, "These human beings have done us such a good deed, how can we return them to their home? They have given us life! Those ducks have been killing us for a long time. Now the brothers have given us back our lives, and we have revived. What can we do to get them back to their own homeland? They have done us such a great service!"

The brothers took their ducks off to one side. They cooked them and feasted a little. They were then told that they would be taken home. The brothers went to the discarded dentalium shells that had been tossed into a huge pile by the dwarves after they had eaten the meat inside. They sorted out the biggest ones they could find. Dentalia are treasures here in our own time. Now the brothers had lots of dentalia.

The dwarves gathered around now and told them: "We are going to return you folks. We shall call the whale who travels all around. He goes by the land that you came from. He will return you to your home. We are going to call him to come here. He has been around for a long time. That whale is an old person!"

So they called the whale, and he came and landed. The people explained that they wanted him to return the two brothers, along with their canoe. They said to Whale, "You can just put them inside where you carry things and take them way over there. You know where they are from."

Whale answered, "Yes, I know where these people are from. I pass by their homeland and I can hear an old woman mourning out loud. She must be their grandmother. Their grandmother mourns. I can see her crying because her grandsons are lost! I will return them."

The canoe was loaded with their dentalia, and then they got on. The whale said to them, "Don't you folks be afraid. You will just be up on top. I will surface, and when I surface you can take a good breath. I shall judge how long I need to surface for you to breathe before I dive again."

The dwarves were happy for the two who were going home.

As they traveled along, night fell. He told them, "I don't want to be seen by a young female. Many people watch as I travel around. I forbid a young female to look at me. If she is menstruating, that is a serious taboo. The minute her eyes were to see me I would go into convulsions and thrash about, in and out of the water!" *He is supernatural!*

They traveled along until they could see a place where there were people living. Whale emerged a little. Suddenly a young woman peeked at him. This bad one peeked at him. She was menstruating. Bad! The minute she set eyes on him, Whale went into convulsions! Everything came spilling out of him—their canoe, their dentalia and the two of them. Somewhere on the other side of Seattle all of their dentalia spilled. The place was called sxʷəbabš before our time.

They managed to get ashore, and they went up on the beach. The whale went away. He went back to where he came from. They felt sad about their dentalia spilling out, they had sorted and gathered so much of it to bring back home. Their spirit powers came to them as they felt sad about all the misfortune they had had to endure.

They arrived there and stopped at a point where there were people living. They were seen by a child who was out playing. With the curiosity of all children {storyteller's aside: "Just like my own grandchildren."} this child went up to them. He knew that his own brothers had been lost at sea. When this child came up to them he was told, "Do not come here. You stand right there. Are you our little brother?"

"Yes. We have been watching for you for a long time. Our people have suffered a lot of hardship and misery since you were lost."

"You go home and tell the people that they are to gather everyone together. We shall go to them only after they have all gathered. We will enter their home then. As soon as we come in we will sing out spirit songs."

The child obeyed and went home and told their people, "My brother is over there. He told me to come and tell you to gather everyone together; then he will come here and come inside."

His people just took him and beat him. {The storyteller's husband chuckles at this point.} They said to the unfortunate child, "You dirty little thing, do you have to say something like that to us?"

The child bravely replied, "My older brother said that to me!"

He ran back to his brothers and told them, "My people just beat me. They think that I am only talking."

"You go ahead and tell them that we are their children who have come. We will go there and go inside only after they have followed our instructions, because we want to sing our spirit songs now."

Again the child ran. "That is my brother who has arrived. Hurry, father, and get everything ready!"

The bad woman who beat him is just his stepmother; his father, however, begins to believe his little son. He has everyone put things in order to welcome those who have been lost.

The brothers then come in from outside. Just as soon as they enter they begin to sing their spirit songs. The mourning cries of the people stop. Instead, they begin to sing the brothers' songs. They sing good spirit songs.

The brothers run from one side of the room to the other. The songs they sing come from out around the water. The power belongs to the salt water tubšadəd, the song of the warrior!

Now things were changed. Deer and other food came down toward the shore. Smelt came out of the water. The shoreline was all white as they came out of the water. They came out and died there. All of the food came freely of its own accord. The bear came along with the other food. That was what happened, and they all sang their spirit songs until everyone's power was strengthened.

That is the end of the story concerning those who were lost.

Coyote Marries His Own Daughter

Told by Martha LaMont at Tulalip in the 1950s

A LOT OF people lived there where Coyote and his daughter lived. Coyote, who was ill, told all of these people: "There is a man from Yakima who wants to marry my daughter. If by chance I should die before this marriage takes place, I want all of you to know that my daughter is to be allowed to marry and go with him when he comes for her."

His people nodded and said, "All right." They all understood his wishes.

Coyote was sick. He had been sick for a long time now. He was sick for a long time, and then suddenly he died.

Just before he died, however, he had instructed his people carefully: "You are to place all of my favorite foods—salmon eggs, dried salmon, dried berries and roots—place them by my body along with a cooking kettle, my dress-up clothes and my face paint. These things are to be placed with me wherever you shall put me after I die." {It was the custom to provide for the spirit as it traveled into the spirit world. Favorite possessions, along with favorite foods were always placed with the body in the burial place.}

Coyote was wrapped in a cattail mat and placed in a canoe after he died. The things he had requested were placed there with him.

Long after his death, children at play down near the water heard a noise. They saw smoke coming from the place where the dead body was. They went closer and saw a fire with a cooking pot such as Coyote had asked for beside it. Thinking that he must be alive, they ventured closer to peek at him. Coyote chased them away: "Go on, get away, you children! I am bad now! I am dead—peeyuwee, hm! I stink! Get away! I have been dead for a long time."

The frightened children ran right home to tell their parents. "We were near Coyote's burial place, and we saw him cooking by a fire. He chased us away and told us that he had been dead for a long time and was a corpse!"

"What business did you children have going there?" The children were spanked, "Don't you go there again!"

But there was Coyote, again pestered by the children. They looked at him. There is smoke rising from a fire and the smell of food coming from the steaming pot beside it. It seems that Coyote is making a soup from the favorite foods he has asked the people to place with his body.

Coyote chased the children, telling them to go away. "Go away, go away! I am spoiled. I am a corpse. I am real bad. I have been dead for a long time. Go on away, children!"

Again the children ran to their parents to tell about this. Again they were spanked and scolded: "Don't you go there again. That is really a corpse you are talking about!"

Time passed. People thought, "After all, he *was* high class." But after a while longer, it was suggested that maybe it would be well for someone to see if the body was where they had put it. Several of the elders went. They saw the body wrapped and lying there. He was most certainly there in the canoe just as he had been left.

But Coyote had just fixed himself and laid himself back down, pretending to be dead. Now he got up again and got himself ready to travel. He prepared himself to go courting his daughter for a wife. He was in love with his daughter and wanted her for himself. How could he manage to get her? He painted his face; then he walked. He wrapped his feet as those from a distance do. He braided his hair and tied it. Then he traveled, looking just like a Yakima would look.

He crossed the little river in front of the village and started hollering across to the people. They heard the stranger but couldn't understand him. As they listened to him, they said to each other, "Maybe he is the man from Yakima who wants to marry Coyote's daughter. Somebody should get a canoe and go across to get him."

When the canoe reached the other shore the stranger was greeted and politely asked where he came from. He replied in a strange language and just slapped at his ears as they tried again to talk to him. He didn't understand.

"We will call Bluejay. Probably she will hear and understand this high-class person who has arrived."

Bluejay, who was fluent in many languages, could indeed understand him. "It seems that this person is the one who is coming for the daughter of Coyote, who is now dead." This is what Bluejay said. "He is the one who has come to marry the daughter of the high-class person who died. You folks should come and greet him."

The people made a decision. "It is best that we abide by the instructions given us by Coyote, who is now dead. Just let the Yakima go ahead and take Coyote's daughter." Following their custom, the people prepared a sleeping area for the man and woman, and they were married.

Not very long after the new groom had been living among his in-laws, the thick layers of face paint he had applied began to dry, and pieces began to break off and fall. Soon his natural face was visible. As he sat where she could see him in the daylight, his daughter knew who it was. "It is that scoundrel father of mine who has made a fool of me."

Coyote's child was now very angry: her thoughts were not good. Now she called upon the guile she had inherited from her father. She said to the village children, "You children will now play outside. You will sing the following words: 'Coyote, Coyote what are you doing to your daughter?' That is what you are to be singing."

The children went—many children. They pounded their drums outside:

"Coyote, Coyote, what are you doing
To your daughter?
Coyote, Coyote, what are you doing
To your daughter?"

Coyote was frightened now, and he said, "Ay! Stop those children! It sounds as if they are naming your father!" *This Yakima* uses fluent Lushootseed when he speaks now. It is just as she had suspected. The dirty thing is her father. He says, "Stop those children. It is your father that they are naming!"

"Honorable one, what is wrong with their game? The children have played like that for a long time." His daughter just got cross with him. She now feels disrespect for him.

Time passed. Now the people said. "What can be done about this?" Coyote again had made fools of all of them. They had gone to the burial place, but Coyote was not there—only the cattail mat and the canoe. "What shall we do to him?"

Thus it was that they did what they did to create a change for him. The people said, "Let us go ahead and walk where we shall walk. We shall walk, and *this* will be frozen: where he is will be frozen. It will become ice, so that it will be impossible for him to get out for a long time. It will just be ice, thick ice, where he will be inside. We shall go ahead and leave him as he sleeps."

The people got ready. It was night time. Then, very early in the morning, it became light. They put a spell on him. His daughter made herself unrecognizable and went outside. Just as she left, the house froze where they were. It was nothing but ice. Not a word was spoken—nothing of any kind. Coyote slept on there. Now the people walked, looking for a place to live. They were ashamed of Coyote. His daughter walked. They went far away.

After several days or so, Coyote woke up: "The dirty things must have put a spell on me! How do I get myself out of this one?" he wondered. "Ha! I could possibly melt the ice enough to peek out and attract someone's attention." So, using his tongue and other warm parts of his body, Coyote worked for several days in order to melt a small hole in the ice. He peeked through; then he began to holler:

"We will travel by water in the morning.
We will travel by water in the morning.
Yes, yes yes, yes, yes, yes!"

Coyote himself hollered all of this for the benefit of listening ears. He is heard by one individual. Raven happened to be flying by and heard him. "Oh, ho! I do believe it is Coyote who is talking!" He came on down to see what Coyote was doing!

As he walked around the house, he could see an eye peeking out through a small opening. *Coyote's eye!* Now Raven thought, "What can I do to him? Maybe I could take his eye away from him!" When Coyote peeked again, Raven took his eye—took it off and took it out. Coyote tried to see who had done this, and Raven took the other eye, too.

Now Coyote was without eyes. There he was! Raven traveled on. Coyote said, "The dirty thing! That Raven has insulted me and taken my eyes!" He was sad to be without them.

Raven went home and bragged to everyone: "I took Coyote's eyes from him. It is very nice the way his eyes are. They seem to sparkle as they fall and roll!"

Some women listening coaxed Raven: "It would be nice of you to give us Coyote's eyes, You had better give them to us, Raven. They are of no importance to you."

Raven got bored with the eyes and said, "Go ahead and take them. Take them."

The women wrapped up the eyes of Coyote and took them away; they walked toward a big village that they knew of.

Meanwhile, Coyote was still there until he finally managed to get out. He managed to wear out the ice and get free.

He began walking, and he came to Snipe and Magpie. They were busy digging roots, but they noticed that Coyote seemed to be confused, bumping into everything as he walked along. He went off to one side and got tangled in a thorny bush. "What is the matter with Coyote? Why is he bumping into that thorny bush?"

Coyote said, "What do you mean? Why, this is what I am looking for. This is the kind of bush that is used for making arrows."

Snipe and Magpie know better: "Oh sure, this kind of thorny bush has long been used for making arrows. That's the kind they use, all right." They continue digging for the special kind of roots they like.

Coyote raised his face and in a loud voice said, "There on the tree is a fat juicy burrowing bug!"

The women said, "Is there really, honorable sir? Just where is it?"

"Right here in front of my eyes. You folks come here and look at it."

Those crazy women, Snipe and Magpie, went. As they approached, Coyote said, "Come closer; right near my hand is where you should look." He had managed to stuff a pair of substitute eyes into his eye sockets, some yellowish-green things that grow on rotten wood in wet slippery ground. He could feel the women come closer.

One of them said to him, "Where?"

He whispered, "You folks look right here on my hand. I will need to hug you to show you just where." He hugged one of them—maybe Snipe—and took her eye from her: then he took her other one. He took out his fake eyes and put on the eyes of this woman. Now Coyote could see very well, and it was she instead who was blind.

"Oh, that dirty thing has made fools of us, as he does to everyone! Now I am going to be blind."

{The storyteller comments in a stylized voice: "Yeah, the high-class one has eyes!"}

"I am just going to travel toward my eyes." It is said that now Coyote started to walk in search of his eyes. As he passed through each village he would stop and ask, "Is there anything that you people know about, any kind of information you can tell me?"

In one place he was told, "It's nothing important, but it is said that some women have the eyes of Coyote, and the people are gathering to watch them!"

"Blast the dirty things that they should have my eyes!" He walked on, and as he went through another village he inquired as before.

Here again he was told: "Nothing much. It is just the eyes of Coyote. It is said that the women have taken them and there is a big gathering because of that."

"Darn the dirty things for having my eyes. I will get even with them for making fun of me by showing my eyes in this manner."

He walked on. He knew that this was the road his eyes had been taken over. Finally as he traveled he came upon an old woman, Illness. She never went anywhere.

Coyote said to Illness, "What are you cooking?"

"Oh, I prepare food for my grandchildren, sir. They also go to the gathering."

"How many grandchildren do you have?"

"I have two grandchildren. There is one older, and there is one younger granddaughter."

"Which way do they go?"

"They go to the eyes of Coyote. People gather there some place. There is a big gathering about that."

Now this made Coyote's thoughts angry! "What can I do to this old woman? Maybe I could kill her."

He walked on a bit, and then he asked his advisers what he should do. They said, "Just look for something to use."

Coyote turned to Illness and said, "I would like to burn you all over!"

Illness replied, "That would be your lucky day when you could do that!"

"I would club you!"

"Ha! You'd have to be pretty lucky to be able to club me!"

Again he turned and walked. He asked. *They* advised him: "Get nettles. Break off nettles and club her all over with them."

Coyote went right away and gathered an armload of nettles. He took them into the home of Illness and told her, "I'm going to sting you all over!"

"šáʔa da da da da da," Illness said. She gave up now. Nettles are her enemy.

After Coyote had thrashed her all over with the nettles, Illness died. He removed her clothes and put them on himself. He would now be disguised as Illness.

There he was. "She" was busy pounding and preparing her granddaughters' food when they got home. She coughed as she pounded.

The younger granddaughter didn't recognize grandma: "Hey! This lady pounds differently!"

"I'm not feeling well is why I do things differently." Then he fed his granddaughters. This food that grandmother has fixed is different. The pieces are left larger. They ate. When they finished, he said to them, "I shall go along with you tomorrow when you go where they are playing."

The elder granddaughter said to the younger, "That would be a good idea, dear, good for your grandmother. We shall take her along. We shall just pack her."

The younger one didn't approve. "What business does she have going to a gathering, when she is Illness!"

"Anyway, she shall go. It's best that she go!"

When morning came they started out. The girls took turns backpacking their grandmother. She never walks, because she is Illness. She coughed and coughed as she was backpacked. Suddenly the younger one threw her down on the ground in anger. *Grandmother* is doing something strange.

The elder asked, "Why did you do that to grandmother?"

The younger one replied, "I don't like what she is doing to me."

So the elder one packs the grandmother most of the time. The younger one is suspicious and senses that it is a stranger, and yet it is dressed like their grandmother. They walked with him for some time before they arrived where the people were gathered to see his eyes.

Then the people said, "?alə hii?! Illness has arrived to look at the eyes of Coyote!" The people were rather startled.

Illness said, "You folks will seat me there at the end where the eyes of Coyote roll. There where they roll."

The eyes of Coyote turn somehow as they roll. Just as people throw them the eyes of Coyote roll, two of them, and they kind of sparkle and flash. They are rather nice to look at as they roll, and they fall there by the one who is throwing them.

Right there they sat her. "Let her be satisfied, your grandmother. Have her there." They sat her there.

He observed for some time; then he whispered to his eyes. His eyes went and landed there where he was. "Oh, my eyes!" He felt bad. Then he said to them, "Come close, my eyes." His eyes stopped: they seemed startled. They didn't roll on immediately. They just landed, and then they again rolled, these eyes of his.

Then he whispered, "Come close, my eyes." His eyes again stopped. They rolled and landed again. When the third time came, he said to them, "Slink over this way, my eyes." His eyes seemed to undulate, and then they went right into his eye sockets. He now threw away these eyes of Magpie's or Snipe's that he was making use of.

Just as he put his eyes on, he was able to see very well, and the grand-daughters said, "Oh, it was that Coyote who made a fool of our grand-mother!"

{The tape ends here. Possibly it was continued on another tape, but it has yet to turn up in the rest of the collection made by Leon Metcalf.}

Eyes of Coyote

Told by Martha LaMont at Tulalip in 1963

THIS IS WHAT was taking place with Coyote and the others: they were all living there together—Coyote and his daughter, Coyote's son-in-law, and Coyote's in-law (the old man who was the father of Coyote's son-in-law). They all lived there together. Coyote's daughter let him stay with them there where they were; and now when it became night there where they were, just as it becomes night every place else, they went to bed, just as everyone else does, and they slept.

Now Coyote got up. He coveted this tool which his in-law used for breaking up and splitting the bark he gathered for firewood. It was sort of like a knife, not like a knife. Rather, it was like rock; rock is the way it was. That was what this one, Coyote, coveted. Oh, but he coveted this tool of his in-law! How could he manage to get it from him? Hatchet is what this is called which was used for splitting wood, bark and other things.

Now it became dark. Coyote went after this hatchet which was used for splitting wood, and he took it from him. Now he belted it on himself, Coyote did; he thought he was stealing. He thought he would go away now, travel. He was going to steal this hatchet which was used for splitting bark. So he took it and he belted it on himself: then he walked. He thought he walked away with it in the night! His daughter, her father-in-law and her husband were all asleep.

He got up and ran away from them, so he thought. He was going to steal this hatchet of his in-law's which he coveted. Then he went. He traveled now, so he thought. But he was mistaken! This in-law of his was aware that something was going on. He knew that something was about to happen.

Anything that belonged to him, however, could not be picked up by anyone other than himself.

He walked now. Coyote thought he had traveled a long way with the hatchet of his in-law belted onto himself. He thought he had gone a long way, but he was just right there in the same place. He just walked around the pit where a fire is usually built. Coyote just walked around there with the hatchet of his in-law belted onto himself. He was stealing it, so he thought! He thought he had gone a long way. "I'm far away some place!" Finally he got tired, so he camped. He thought he camped, because he was so tired, finally, after walking, traveling so far; then he camped. He sat, then lay down there where he camped. However, right next to the fire where his daughter was, was where he was lying down camping. He hadn't gone anywhere, because he had had a spell put on him concerning this thing he was stealing. The owner had caused a change. Nobody could steal it. Nobody could do anything with it, because the hatchet was his! Then Coyote took the hatchet and belted it on.

Now his daughter, her husband and her father-in-law woke up. "What in the world is your father doing, what? He is lying there, right near the fire!" The hatchet which he had belted on was plainly visible. They saw him. "Why, oh why, does he do that?"

His daughter said to him, "Why do you belt on the hatchet which belongs to your in-law, my father, why? Untie that which you have fastened to yourself. Why have you done that to the hatchet of your in-law?"

"Oh, my daughter, it is just because of my concern for its safety that I strap it to myself," Coyote just said. However, he was embarrassed because he was stealing and because he was still there in the same place, it seemed. He hadn't gone anywhere. He hadn't managed to travel a great distance, because the owner of the hatchet which was used for splitting bark had created a spell over him. He took it and untied and put down this thing which he wished to steal.

Night came again. Again night came. Coyote repeated what he had been doing. He took it, belted it on and walked, so he thought. He thought that he had walked a long distance, but he just walked round and round their firepit. He didn't go anywhere. He was just there where his daughter lived, where her fire was.

Again his daughter woke up. There was her father again lying there. He still had his in-law's hatchet belted onto himself. Her husband complained to her: "Why does your father do what he does, why? Here he lies again!"

Again she went and kicked her father. "Why do you take the hatchet of your in-law, why? Untie it and go away."

He got up, and—"Oh, it is just because I am afraid for it that I belt it on, afraid that it might be taken by someone who might come here to us." {Coyote uses stylized speech here—baby talk.} He untied it again and put it down.

Maybe it was three times that he stole the hatchet when his daughter, who was feeling embarrassment for her father in front of her husband and father-in-law, now made a decision. (She was ashamed that her husband would have to be the one to keep her father from stealing.) She was ashamed of her father. So she said to her husband and her father-in-law, "I guess the only thing we can do is to leave this person who used to be my father. We will just leave him, and we will make a change happen now. You will create a spell—you, my father-in-law—and where he is will freeze. Where we are. It will freeze! It will be ice, all of it! And there will be no place for him to go outside after we have gone out. Let him be stranded right there! What will he do?"

So they walked; and, just as soon as they did so, it froze as they went outside. It was that very night, then, that it froze for them, because they had advised Coyote to go ahead and cover himself up with a blanket and sleep. Then they left him. They walked. Where?

He woke up! This Coyote woke up. Then he found out: "Oh! This is just ice now where I am! My daughter must have left me! There is no place where I can go outside. I can't do anything. Everything is ice!" He was unable to go anywhere, so there he was! "I have had a change happen to me. I guess I must have behaved unforgivably." There he was, and now what would he do? What would Coyote do? This is what he thought to himself: "What will I do?"

Then he thought: "Oh! I guess I could holler. I could holler. I could pretend to be hollering at someone there, walking nearby some place." Now Coyote pretended to be hollering at someone there inside of the ice:

"We are going by water in the morning,
We are going by water in the morning,
Oh yes, yes indeed, yes, yes."

(It was he himself who was agreeing with himself.) He pretended to have lots of people there. But he was all alone inside of the ice.

Now Raven heard him. Raven was doing something. Raven was out traveling when he heard him. "What is the matter with Coyote that he says what he is saying, what?"

It froze now. Everywhere was frozen. Then Coyote managed somehow to be able to make a hole in the ice. He did something to it. He licked the ice with his tongue until it got thin. He warmed his tongue on parts of his body and caused the ice to get thin. He just seemed to know how much to do in order to be able to see out; then he did that. He continued. He continued until he could peek outside. Then, possibly after several days, he managed to do it: he made a hole through. It was just big enough for him to peek through with one eye, and he peeked with one eye as he hollered:

"We are going by water in the morning,
We are going by water in the morning,
Oh yes, yes indeed, yes, yes!"

Where is someone saying this? Now Raven heard him. It seems he was the only one traveling about (whatever form he was in—because Raven was also different). Then he went and heard where the sound was coming from there. Then he saw! "Oh! There is a peeper, it seems. Here he peeks!" Then Raven pecked out the eye of this poor unfortunate thing! His eye was pecked and taken out. The little eye was taken. He peeked with the other eye, and it was pecked. It was taken. Now Coyote was blind. He was without eyes when they were pecked out.

Raven took them away. He announced that he had stolen them from Coyote. Now Raven was cornered by these women. There were two women who cornered him. They took them away from him. Now these women took the eyes of Coyote, and they walked away with them.

There is Coyote where he is. What will the poor thing, who is now blind, do? Now, possibly, he managed to do something; then he, Coyote, managed to get out. It got bigger, this which he made for himself to be able to get out through.

Now these women who had stolen his two eyes went. They made a place for people to come. As the women passed by the people who lived there, the people asked what it was that they had. They replied, "Oh, we have taken Coyote's eyes away from him." They went on.

Different ones asked, "What do you have there?"

"Oh, it is the belongings of Coyote that we have." They went. These were polite words which were spoken! Again they were asked. They said, "It is Coyote's eyes that we are making fun of."

These insults hurt Coyote's feelings. Now he knew: this was what had happened to his eyes!"

The women took them. They arrived with them at their grandmother's place. Their grandmother was old Illness. She was the germ which carries the coughing illness. She was a live old woman, yet she was illness, sickness. She didn't usually do anything, go anywhere. She just stayed there, coughing. This was the grandmother of these young women. They made a house for their grandmother. They made a place for people to gather way over there. It was nice—maybe like a meadow was the way it was. It was nice, very nice, round. Now they made a place to roll the eyes of Coyote. They made a place for people to gather.

They went then and tried the eyes of Coyote. They rolled them. The eyes went. They kind of sparkled, these two eyes. And they rolled them that way.

The people found out about this then, and they gathered. They watched. The eyes kind of sparkled when they rolled. Then the people said,

"ʔalə hay. . . .
Do you folks see
The eyes of Coyote?"

This is what they hollered for the eyes when they were rolling. Then the eyes landed one place and then again they landed. Rolling. They sort of had a place made for them to roll. And lots of people were watching. These eyes of Coyote were good to watch.

Another day. Again the people gathered for it. Another day. Again the people gathered. The eyes of Coyote! When they were rolled, the people screamed and hollered:

"ʔalə hay . . . ,
    The eyes of Coyote!
ʔaləhay . . . !"

This is what they hollered for the eyes. When they landed at one end, they came back again to the other end. Lots of people! It was an event for a big gathering!

Now Coyote traveled, and he questioned the people. They said, "No, there is nothing of importance going on. Only some women took Coyote's eyes and somewhere probably they have gathered the people to see them."

They got themselves in trouble right there, the foolish no-goods. "You'll find out when I get to where my eyes are," Coyote said about them to himself.

He went, and again he found people who lived there. "Have you folks noticed anyone passing by here?"

"Yes. Someone went by here, Sir, but I guess it was the things of Coyote that they were taking, and I guess that is what they are gathering about over that way," they answered.

Oh, now, this answer was acceptable to his mind. He didn't get angry. He felt good about this reply. Then he went on. He probably asked several more, and again he said to someone, "What went by here? Do you folks know?"

"Yes. It is said that the women took the eyes of Coyote and that is what the people are gathering about. There is great merriment over the eyes of Coyote!"

This is how they get in trouble in his mind. "You folks will find out when I travel. I will get my eyes!"

Now he arrived at the house of this old woman as he traveled, the grandmother of these individuals who are having the gathering way over there. And they have something which is watched by many. Many people gather there! Now Coyote says, "What are your grandchildren doing?" (The next sentence on the tape recording is unintelligible.) There are two grandchildren of the old woman, Illness. And this Coyote said to her, "What are they doing?"

"Oh, they went because they have the eyes of Coyote there. That is what the big gathering is about way over there at the big meadow. They roll them!"

Now he had arrived. He had arrived at the old woman's, and he had asked her what she was doing. He planned to kill the old woman, this Coyote. He would club her to pieces, this Illness. "I will sting you all over!"

"ʔa daʔ daʔ daʔ daʔ. That would be your lucky day, when you could sting me all over!"

"I will take you, and I will knock you into the hot fire!"

"No! It would be only luck if you ever knocked me down."

He went outside, then, and he consulted someone sort of the way he is, his strength. And his younger brothers just said to him, "You would just say as usual (You are so clever!) that you had already planned to take those nettles over there and break them and hit her all over with them, and that would cause her death."

"Oh, I knew that all the time, my little brothers!" He went and came to the nettles, and he brought them in, and he stung the old woman all over with them.

"ʔa daʔ daʔ daʔ daʔ," the old woman just said as she died.

Now he took the old woman's clothing. The old woman's clothing just drooped—her clothing, kind of like her hide, whatever it was. He took his own off and put on the clothing of this Illness, her hide or whatever it was. This Coyote was now going to be kind of just like this old woman had been as she sat.

Because now the women who were having the gatherings over the playthings had arrived. His eyes: This is what he was going to sneak after. They arrived. Their grandmother had been killed.

The old woman who was coughing was pounding their food. And the youngest, younger than the others, said, "Say, you are pounding differently, grandmother. Different now. Different from your customary way, you are doing!"

"It is just because I am not feeling well that I do it this way, my granddaughter. It is just because I don't feel well." (Here it was because it was Coyote doing it that it was different.)

The youngest one suspected something. The older sister said, "Don't say anything to your grandmother. Why do you have to speak harshly to her when maybe she is just not feeling well?" There they are. Now he fed them. And when he fed them, because he had asked old Illness, he knew that the eldest was first, and her sister was after her, and the very youngest was the very last. The food she was fed was different. There were three of them. {The next sentence is unintelligible on the tape.}

Now they said, "Say, our grandmother seems to have pounded our food good."

"It is because I don't feel well."

However, they found her strange; they didn't recognize her as their accustomed grandmother, because she was doing this differently, because she was different! (But their grandmother had been killed, and this one was just dressed the way the old one used to be.)

Now Illness said, "What happens at the gathering?"

"Oh, it is nice. There are lots of people who gather there."

"You will take me along with you tomorrow, my grandchildren. You folks will take me now. I would like to see what the eyes of Coyote do."

"We shall backpack our grandmother. We shall pack her. We shall just take turns with her. You will go along." Then they prepared themselves, and they went again when day came. Then one of them packed her grandmother. When her weight became a burden, it would be another one's turn. They took her a long, long way before they let another one pack her.

Later now. Then: "Grandmother is doing something different!" Now the youngest one got angry. "What is the matter with you, grandmother? You keep backing up, and I have a hard time trying to pack you. Keep kind of up high; then I can pack you better." And she went lower, backing up, this one. But here it was this Coyote. It was not their own grandmother. He was just dressed up in the clothing that had belonged to the old woman. They found her strange, yet they continued to pack her.

"What are you saying to your grandmother? Leave her alone," the eldest one said. And then she carried her, even though her grandmother did the same thing to her. The eldest one didn't do anything about it. She just enjoyed carrying her grandmother, the one who just kept backing up that way. And she carried her.

Then: "Carry your grandmother!" Again the youngest one carried the grandmother, and she backed herself up, and she really went backing up to her. Sort of like a man now was what she did to her granddaughter.

Then: "Hey! What is the matter with this no-good grandmother, that she is so changed now?" And she is thrown down on the ground!

"Why do you do that to your grandmother, why do you?" She groaned and coughed. The eldest took her again, backpacked her and took her. She hadn't walked very far with her when again she repeated her action, only the eldest didn't say anything: she just seemed to like what her grandmother did. She backed up, and it was kind of like what a man does that she did to her granddaughter. Yet she took her on. Further on she again said, "It will be you now who shall pack your grandmother."

Now the old lady said, "It would be best if you would seat me at the end where the eyes of Coyote roll. I will be at the one end, where his eyes land when they roll them. That would be best. It will be good for me to be near the eyes."

So they took her where she was going to be seated. Just as soon as they got her there, they started. The people sang for Illness:

"ʔaləhay . . . Illness has been brought here;
She has come to watch the eyes of Coyote,
ʔaləhay . . ."

(These words were sung out in chorus by all of the people in this gathering.) It was because Illness never went anywhere, and here she had come to watch the eyes of Coyote!

"You will have me at the end." Yes, it was there that they sat her, and she coughed. Then his eyes were rolled. Yes, his eyes sort of sparkled. So nice to look at! So many ways it was nice to look at. It was kind of like that which is called the rainbow, is the way it was.

Then, right away, he whispered to his eyes, "Come near, my eyes, come near." His eyes stopped there. They stopped when he whispered to them. Then again they went rolling.

"ʔaləhay. The eyes of Coyote
Stop when they come
To the old woman, Illness."

But he had caused them to turn a little when he whispered to them. He just tested, only. Again his eyes went rolling. Those at the other end said,

"Ɂaləhay, the eyes of Coyote, Ɂaləhay . . ."

They enjoyed them because they were wonderful to watch! Again they were rolled. Again he whispered to his eyes, "Come closer, my eyes." His eyes rolled closer to him. Again the crowd sang for them, and they went again!

"Ɂaləhay . . . ,
The eyes of Coyote pause
Near the old woman, Illness,
Over there."

Here it was Coyote who was doing this. Now it comes to the time that the song caused him anger, and those at the other end got in trouble when they sang out,

"Ɂaləhay . . . The eyes of Coyote, Ɂaləhay"

Then they landed where he was, and—"Come closer, my eyes; you will come closer!" Then truly his eyes did go closer to him, and they rolled. They went. The people sang again for them. They stopped at the old woman.

"ɁaləhayɁ, the eyes of Coyote."

He wanted to try his eyes out again before he called them. They were rolled. They came! They landed where the old woman was.

"Ɂaləhay, the eyes of Coyote stop
When they get close
To the old woman, Illness."

Here it is because he said, "Come close, my eyes." Then suddenly he whispered to his eyes, "Go in where you belong, my eyes!" The worthless substitutes which he had been using were those red sort of rotten things which stick to logs in the winter. They are sort of reddish, kind of a fungus, red. These were the substitutes that Coyote had been using. They were the ones which fell down. His eyes went in where they belonged! The people were just dumbfounded.

As soon as his eyes were in place, Coyote stood up, and the clothes of the old woman, Illness, fell down. They collapsed downward. They fell right away. Then the one whose grandmother this had been said, "We really found her a stranger as we backpacked her. But my sister reprimanded me. She said this was her grandmother. I thought all along that something must have happened to my grandmother, and that that was why this one was acting strange."

Now Coyote went and said to the people, "So! The high class people have my eyes for playthings! They make fun of my eyes!" Then he turned around, and he caused a fog to descend over the people. It was his own urinator which he waved over them as he turned around! Then the people were buried in the fog.

He walked on. "So the high class people have fun with the eyes of Coyote!" He went.

"Oh, oh! So it was Coyote who came to us. He got his eyes!" There the people were, and they became confused because they were fogged in. They couldn't go anywhere. They just stumbled around, bumping their faces into things there. It fogged and fogged. He made it that way. Retribution! This was how he got even with them.

He went then and returned, and he did the same as he traveled. These were the people that he wanted to do in, wanted to change. He came to those whom he had first asked, and he changed them, made them worthless. He asked people if they knew about anything.

They said that it was said that Coyote was coming. "He is coming." He came. They had heard about him. Now they planned. "We shall tell him to go from the top of the last house!" They made a huge fire of fir bark.

Then he asked, "Where can I get in? Everything is closed up."

"From the roof where the smoke goes, honorable sir. That is the only door that we have now."

This Coyote, he got himself up high, and he tried to get in through the place where the smoke from the fire goes. The fire was burning hard. Then he came down now. Coyote landed right in the fire, and they said about him, "Bring a forked stick, and we will jab him all over." Then they poked Coyote's neck into the fire, until it was only his nose that was alive. It is now just the nose of Coyote that is left to howl today in the world that the people know today. That was not the way Coyote used to be when he was first a Coyote.

Now the people evolved, and they became worthless; they changed. When he came to another house, he would say to them, "You will be just this way now." He would change them! It was wrong for them to make fun of his eyes. But the nice people were spared. "Those of you with kind, good thoughts will be the way you are for the coming generations." He didn't change them. He changed things as he traveled, this Coyote—because he was different, too. He changed the other ones. What did he do to them until it ended?

That is the end.

Basket Ogress

Told by Martha LaMont at Tulalip in 1968

BASKET OGRESS SPOKE to her little daughter, Tree Roots. "Little Roots, I want you to build a fire and heat those rocks. We are going to have tender roasted children for our supper!"

Basket Ogress put her huge clam basket on her back and hurried down to the water where the little children were playing. She grabbed them all up and stuffed them into her basket. Little Hunchback kept wriggling himself up over the children. He managed to be at the top of the basket as Ogress lumbered upland thinking about her supper.

Little Hunchback saw a tree branch that was hanging sideways. He grabbed ahold of it and swung himself out of the basket as Ogress crawled under with her pack. Then he ran. He went home. When he got there he told how the bad Basket Ogress had stolen the children. The people immediately prepared themselves to go and rescue them. They would *kill* that Ogress!

When Basket Ogress arrived home with her basket full of children, she took them out and seated them around the fire. As she thought about her dinner, she began to sing and dance.

She sang:

The children will now be roasted,
The children will now be roasted,
The children will now be roasted!

Around the fire she went. It was a great big fire, and her daughter, little Tree Roots, had lots of rocks heating there. Ogress was very happy. She was glad because now she had lots of tender little children to eat! She became slightly dizzy as she danced around the fire, and she staggered just a little. Oh, but she was so happy as she thought about the dinner she would have in just a little while. It was such a big, hot fire!

The older boys and girls noticed how she had staggered as she danced. They whispered to each other, "*She* could burn! We could push the dirty thing, because she gets dizzy when she dances and staggers toward the fire. We could push her down and push her neck onto the fire with a forked stick! We could all poke her and hold her down on the fire. We could manage to kill her. It would be a good thing if she died, anyway!"

The children discussed their plan; then one of them ran and brought back a forked stick. They said to little Tree Roots, "Little Tree Roots, go and get a forked stick so that we can get your mother out of the fire if she should get dizzy and fall there." Little Tree Roots went and returned with the good forked stick that they used when they were out hunting.

Now they watched carefully as Basket Ogress happily danced around her big hot fire. As soon as she staggered just a little, they pushed her toward the fire and poked her neck onto the hot rocks with the forked sticks. She thrashed around for a little while. Then she died in the fire! They kept her pressed onto the fire. Basket Ogress, the monster who liked to eat children, died! She would have eaten them if she had not been killed herself.

It was little Hunchback who ran and told. Then the people came. They made certain that she was truly dead. There was still a little life left in her when the relatives of the children arrived, so they completely killed her. She died!

After Basket Ogress was dead they covered her over with ashes and left her there. Her little daughter, Tree Roots, left. She walked at first, but then she went running away from the place where her mother had died.

skúbx, the younger sister of Basket Ogress, had been hunting far away from home. Now she quietly returned. As she glanced around the area, she noticed that a big fire had died down, but there appeared to be something there covered with ashes. Then she chuckled to herself and said, "Well, well! As usual, the great, powerful one has her game cleverly hidden. This is probably her game that she has roasted and hidden here." She went closer to investigate what was covered at the fire. She knew it had been roasted. She uncovered part of it. True! It was cooked and falling apart, it was so well done! This younger sister had been out hunting and hadn't had time to stop and cook herself a good meal. She was so hungry. Now she ate. She thought that this was some game that her sister had cooked and left covered at the fire.

After she had eaten her fill she began to feel a little sick, and she said, "Oh, my goodness, this tastes like it might have been the dear one!" She realized now that it was her own sister whom she had eaten. She got scared and went away from there.

She walked a long way until she came to some people in a village. She asked them, "Where is your door?"

They answered, "It is through the roof that people enter who come here." They already knew, however, that Basket Ogress' sister would be traveling, and they had built a huge fire beneath the roof. When skúbx came through the hole in the roof, they threw her into the fire, where she died.

Now both monsters were dead, and that is why there are no monsters here on top, the way the world is now. They would still be here if they hadn't been killed in the fire, the bad Basket Ogress and her younger sister. The younger sister was also bad. This story is about the way it was in the beginning. Those monsters liked to eat children. They killed them. They didn't eat old people, just the children.

The daughter of Basket Ogress, little Tree Roots, lived. Coming generations will now be all right, because the monsters were killed.

That is the end.

Legend of the Seasons

Told in English by Harry Moses in 1952

MANY PEOPLE LIVED there in a small village. The Head Man of this village lived there in the middle. He had a daughter. Another family in the village had a son. This young man wanted to marry the daughter of the Head Man, but the Head Man disapproved, because the boy and his family were poor. The young couple got together anyway! The girl's father was furious, and he planned a way to get rid of his son-in-law.

He built a big cedar box, and he put the young man into this box. It was early in the spring when this girl's father put the box into the water. It was about April. The box drifted now for one moon (a month). The young man's parents and all of his relatives worried and looked for him. After the box drifted for one month, it came to the salt water and beached on the shore of a little island.

An old woman lived on this island with three younger women—a housekeeper, a cook and a dishwasher. The women had been on this island since the beginning of time. One day the old woman told her servants that they would go out for a walk together along the beach. Pretty soon they saw this big box there. The old woman sent her servants back for a tool to open it, because it was closed tight to keep the water out. When they came back with an axe, they got busy and took the top off. There was a young man! The women took him out of the box, and he went home with them.

He told them his story. The women felt sorry when he told them how he had been treated. The weather was getting warm now. It was about in July when the women told the young man to get himself ready. He was going to go home to see his mother and father. He was carefully instructed, because he was far away from his own territory. The women got ready to go along with him. Before they left the house, they gave him some small nuts. Four of them. Two were put into his left pocket and two in his right pocket. The old woman told him that he was not to show the nuts to his people until four days had passed. Then the women disappeared!

After traveling for some time, the man came to the place where the women had instructed him to beach the boat. He then walked for a long time, but he finally came to his own village. His mother and father were home. They were old now, and they had given up looking for their son. When someone knocked at their door, they opened it. There stood something shining so bright, like the sun, that they couldn't see it. Finally, as their eyes got accustomed to the light, they could see that this was a person. They asked, "Who are you?"

The young man said, "It's me, your son. I have come home!" Slowly he explained everything that had happened to him. His parents knew then that it was really their lost son. The old man hurried out to tell the other villagers of his son's return. The people all rushed over to share the happiness of the old people—even the Head Man!

He examined the young man carefully and recognized him as the one he had put adrift in the tightly closed big cedar box. It was the same man, but yet he was different. He was so bright, he was shining! The Head Man immediately asked him to come back to his daughter. The young man said no!

Parents of other young women asked him to be their son-in-law. He said no! The Head Man coaxed him for three days to take his daughter. Still the young man said no!

Toward the end of the third day, the young man reached into his left pocket, took out a nut and rolled it over the house floor. When the nut quit rolling, it stopped; and there stood a beautiful young woman. She was shining so brightly that at first no one could look at her. The Head Man looked at this beautiful woman, and he continued to urge the young man to marry his daughter!

The young man reached into his pocket, took out another nut and rolled it over the floor. When it stopped rolling, there stood a woman even prettier than the first one. The Head Man looked at her and still urged the young man to take his daughter! Again he refused!

He reached into his right pocket, took out another nut and rolled it. There stood another young woman, more beautiful than the rest! Why did the Head Man want the son of the poor old man to marry his daughter, when the son already had three beautiful women?

The young man reached into his pocket and took out the last nut. He rolled it, and it became another beautiful woman! It was the old woman. She stood there and looked at the other three beautiful girls standing in the room. She looked at the young man and sternly said, "I instructed you that you were to wait four days before you revealed us to your people."

When the young man turned around to explain his impatience, the women were all gone. They had disappeared!

The village people felt sad for the young man, but he just said, "Don't worry! I am going to go and try to find my wives."

He walked. He walked east for a long time until he came to a mountain. Near the top of the mountain he could see an old man. This old man had been sitting there since the world first began. He was smoking a long stone pipe. The young man asked him, "Where is your home? Why are you sitting here?"

The old man replied, "I've been sitting here since the world first began, smoking my pipe." He puffed on his long pipe, and the young man could see clouds and fog rise from the bowl of this pipe.

He walked on. He walked for a long time, until he came to an old woman who lived there in a big old house. The young man asked her, "Are you all alone here?"

She answered, "No, I have a grandson who is out enjoying himself." The old woman then invited him to stay, and they would have supper together when her grandson came home. She had been sewing when the young man came in. Now she removed her thimble from her finger and she placed it on the fire. She poured some water into the thimble, took three beans and placed them into the water in the thimble.

The young man watched this and he thought, "How can three little beans cook in a thimble, and how can that be enough for three people to eat for supper?" The old woman could read the man's thoughts, but she said nothing.

When her grandson came home, the old woman took the thimble from the fire, and she put the food on the table. As they were eating, the grandson told them that he had been in a horse race with many horses racing. His horse was a small one. He said that they had raced and jumped over a fire! As he talked they all ate the beans that were in the thimble. They ate and ate, and the thimble never got empty!

Now the young man told the old woman and her grandson his story. He told them about being put into the big cedar box and everything that had happened to him. He told them about the beautiful women and the nuts. The woman's grandson advised this young man to keep going in the direction that he had been traveling.

So, he walked. He continued to walk until he came to three boys who were on top of a mountain. These boys had been quarreling since the beginning of time. Their oldest brother had died, and they were quarreling about his coat. This coat made the wearer invisible! One brother shouted: "I want the coat! I am the oldest!" Another one screamed: "No, it is mine!" The youngest whined: "I want the pretty coat!"

He stopped walking and he listened to these young men. Then he asked, "What are you doing?"

They answered, "Our oldest brother died, and this coat belonged to him. We are trying to decide who should have it."

He said to them, "You must earn this coat." He told them, "I will take this ball to the top of the mountain, and I will roll it. Whichever one of you touches it before it gets down to the bottom is the one who will have the coat!"

He took the ball up to the top of the mountain, and he rolled it. All of the boys chased after it, but not one of them could manage to touch it! He told them, "None of you touched it."

The boys brought the ball back up the mountain, quarreling as they climbed. "I'm the one who touched it!" "No, I'm the one!" The man took the ball from them, and again he rolled it down. They chased it. No! Still nobody touched it.

Now, the fourth time, the boys chased after the ball, and the man went over and put the coat on. He disappeared! He was invisible!

The boys climbed back up the mountain, carrying the ball. They were arguing as they climbed. The man stood there and listened to them as they quarreled. When it came time, they were going to give the ball back to the man so he could roll it down the hill. He wasn't anywhere around there!

They couldn't see him! They turned to each other and asked, "Where is that man?" While they were doing this, the man walked away.

He walked until he came to an old lady living in a great big old house. She was cold and shivering.

The young man asked her, "Are you all alone?"

She answered, "No, I have four grandsons, but they are not here right now."

The young man asked her, "What do you do?"

She answered, "I just sit here." Then she told the young man, "You wait. One of my grandsons will be home in a little while. My grandsons are powerful! You will freeze when they come home. You had better hide over there in the corner, and I will cover you with these skins, and you'll keep warm." The old woman began to shiver as she talked. He shivered, too. She told him: "My oldest grandson is coming home. His name is December."

December came to the door, and he stood there and said, "Gramma, it smells like a person in here!"

His grandmother replied, "No, I'm all alone here."

Then December said, "Gramma, I traveled from the north; and as I came, the ground froze, and the people got cold, and their fingers dropped off, and their ears dropped off, and they froze. The trees twisted and broke, and the water became ice, and it snowed!"

When her grandson finished telling his story, he walked way back to the south of the house, and there he stood.

The old woman whispered to the young man, "My grandson January will be coming home in just a little while." She began to shiver with the cold, and so did he.

January came to the door, and he spoke to his grandmother, "Gramma, it smells like a person in here!"

She answered: "No one has been here!"

January told his grandmother of all the things he had done as he traveled. He said, "I twisted the trees and I broke them. I froze the people and the ground and the water." When he finished telling his story, he went to the back of the room, and he stood with his brother.

Again, the old woman and the young man began to shiver. The old woman whispered to him, "Another grandson will be home soon. He's powerful, too!"

February came to the door. His hair stood up all over his head, and he looked wild and mean! He stood there and said to his grandmother, "It smells like a person in here!"

She answered, "No, there is no one here!"

February told her, "I made great freezing rains fall all over the people. Mountains slid into the rivers! Forests fell before me!" When he finished talking, he went to the back of the house, and he stood there with his brothers.

The old woman told the young man, "My youngest grandson will be home soon. He is not dangerous."

March came to door, and the old woman felt warmer. When he entered the house, March turned to his grandmother and said, "It smells like a person in here."

Grandmother replied, as she usually did, "No, I'm here by myself!"

March came in and told his grandmother, "I have been traveling for a long way behind my brothers. They have been killing people with the cold. I have been healing things with warmth. I thawed the ground so things can grow."

The young man began to feel nice and warm, so he threw off the skins. When March saw him, he asked, "What are you doing Are you going some place? Are you looking for something?" March had such an understanding voice, the young man told him of all the troubles he had endured and of his travels as he searched for his wives.

March listened, and then he told the young man about a woman who was preparing to be married. He said, "There is going to be a big dinner and a party at that place. If you hurry, maybe you can get there in time. You should go in that direction."

The young man walked and walked, and finally he arrived at the village. He put on his magic coat; then he went to the door. He could see lots of people in there, and many women were working at the large table. He could see his wife from the island sitting there with the man she was about to marry. She was so pretty. She sat there and kept talking to the man that she was going to marry. She talked and she ate. There were lots of people eating with them.

He reached over her shoulder and drank her herb-tea! When she saw her empty cup, she spoke to her servant: "You didn't give me any herb-tea!"

The servant filled her cup. He drank it. Again she called for some herb-tea. After the third time, she began to suspect. Maybe her first husband was doing this to her. He was smart!

She went into her sleeping room, and she came out with a very powerful tube, which she put up to her eye. She looked around, but she couldn't see anything. She did this a second time with a more powerful tube, and still she couldn't see anyone. The fourth time, she used a tube that was still more powerful. Then she saw her husband! She went to him and hugged him.

They went back to his people, and they lived a happy life together. He found his wife in the month of April.

The Legend of the Humpy Salmon

Told by Ray Paul at Swinomish in 1981

{While giving this story, Ray Paul alternated between Lushootseed and English. To indicate this, the Lushootseed is translated directly and his own English version is given between brackets.}

THERE WAS THAT one who was a Humpy. He was an old Humpy. He was a man. And this young woman admired him.

{This old Humpy. This young lady saw him, and she took a liking to him, and she got together with him.}

Now they swam upriver, where they were from. It was their own river, where they will swim, where they will return.

{But he is going to go back to the river where he come down from when he was young. They swam and swam together with this young woman. She stayed right with him. She wouldn't leave him at all.}

She didn't leave this man she admired. Then they swam. Soon, they neared this river where they came from. But he sensed that his body was getting weak.

{That's his body began to get soft! The salt water it will wash off of the fish. That's what makes the salmon strong, the salt water. Then he began to know he was getting weak. His girlfriend would look at him, and he was still all right, and then they kept swimming up the river. Further up the river he went, the more that salt water washed off him, and he got really weak after that.}

His body was getting weak.

{Then his young woman left him.}

Now this young Humpy woman who had been keeping him company began to find him offensive.

{It was a young Humpy lady.}

This young woman left this old man. There he was, all alone swimming, as he swam upriver.

{He was all alone going up the river now.}

Suddenly he saw some young women. These young women just looked at him and scorned him, and he went on swimming upriver. This old man was scorned!

{They thought he looked so old, and they didn't like him, so they swam away from him and went up the river. Then he had to swim up the river all alone again, until he ran into some more young girls. Again they just saw him, and they swam away from him. He looked really old, now!}

Now this Humpy man began to change.

{This old Humpy got old so fast because that fresh water will get a salmon old really quick. They don't last very long, because the salt water washes off from them.}

He looks spawned out; he gets red, that one does. Then it was that he gave up. "Oh, maybe I should turn around and return to the ocean, and my body would get strong.

{His body would get strong, he thought, if he got to the salt water again. He did turn, and he went back down the river, and he ran into some more young girls, and they just swam away from him. They didn't like him because he was really old now, just about swimming. He got down the river, and—}

The elders would say he just drifts. He just drifted along. He went. He went, always swimming toward the middle. He arrived at the ocean, and he found out that he was really very weak now.

{He found out he's going to get weak. He got out to the salt water too late to toughen his body over again. And he kept swimming, swimming, until he got out to the ocean. Then he really gave up.}

He immediately went and turned. Now instead it was his stomach that was floating on top. That is the end of that one.

{That old Humpy, he just got out to the ocean, and he "bellied up," and he couldn't swim any more. He died, belly up!}

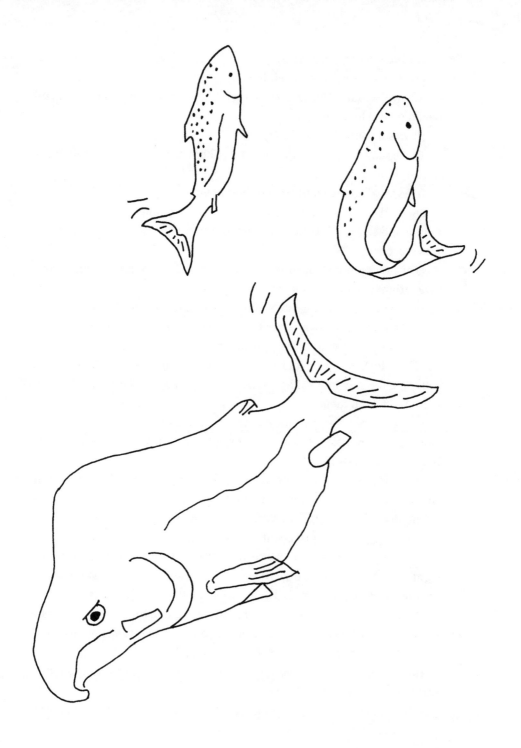

{At his point a listener commented, "Here he had been such a handsome man, admired by the young women!"}

Ray added: "You see, the further up the fish goes up the river, they get old quick. That fresh water will do that. All that salt water washes off from their body. Once that salt water washes off from them, they'll get soft and get old really fast. They'll get red. So the salt water has a lot to do with our wild life, salt water life out in the ocean. Like that story there about the salmon. They go up the river. If they don't get up the river soon enough, they'll die before they spawn."

The Work of the Winds

Told by Ray Paul at Swinomish in 1981

SOUTH WIND HAS special duties to perform. He has work that has to be done regularly for the earth.

After all of the plants and trees have formed their seeds, South Wind takes these children and shakes them off the limbs and branches. He blows hard so they will fall to the earth. He blows the rain over them. In this way he plants the children. They sink into the ground. South Wind watches carefully as the children begin to grow in the warm weather. He sees that they are not very strong, so he knows that they have to have some exercise to make them stronger. South Wind blows hard to exercise the babies. Now they get stronger!

He is doing his work in order for the plants and trees to mature and bear fruit. Now he blows a warm wind to ripen the fruit. This is his work!

When the season of the year changes, South Wind looks at the plants and trees. If the children are still hanging onto the limbs and branches, again he blows them. If he doesn't blow them down and into the ground, they will freeze and they will die! If he doesn't plant them in the warm ground, we will have no more trees and bushes.

North Wind frowns upon this work. He is not as loving as South Wind. He crossly blows South Wind. Blows and blows him. East Wind comes along and helps his friend blow.

South Wind backs up when he realizes that he himself could be overcome by the cold! North Wind and East Wind blow him until he backs up. He backs up until he is right back where he comes from.

Again the earth becomes warm. South Wind gently blows at North Wind until North Wind becomes discouraged and goes away!

This is the work of the winds. The End.

The Legend of the Three Sisters {sqíʔqiʔqaʔ}

Told by Ray Paul at Swinomish in 1981

OUR ANCESTORS CALLED this "The Story of the Three Sisters" when they used to tell it.*

These dear little sisters were out walking. They were walking toward the east, when suddenly the eldest stopped and told her sisters what was on her mind: "Oh, how can we manage to find the Creator?"

The youngest sister, who always seemed to be the brightest, quickly replied, "We could build a great big, tall house that reached up to the heavens!"

The older sisters agreed that this would be a good thing to do, so they began to build. In just a few days they had built it quite high. They put a door there on the east side. They finished the first story.

The sisters began building their second story, and again they put a door on the east side. When the eldest one opened it, she could look down and see that they were way, way up in the sky now. But they were not high enough yet.

They built yet another story and put a door on the east side. They didn't know that God was watching them through the door that was on the north side. The eldest one looked down, but now she couldn't see the earth, because they were too far up in the sky. Quickly she closed the door. The door on the north side opened, and a voice asked them what they were

---

* sqíʔqiʔqaʔ means "little younger sisters" in Lushootseed.

doing. They didn't know that it was God who was asking, "What are you folks doing?"

They answered, "Oh, we want to get up high enough to reach our Creator. We want to reach God!" They were not aware they were talking to Him.

Now the Creator said to them, "I want you girls to get in a row, and I want you to follow me." The sisters obeyed and turned and walked through the door on the north side of their home. He lined them up there and instructed them: "You girls will sit down right here."

The youngest girl turned to her sisters and said, "I wonder what is going to be done with us and why we have been told to do this." They didn't know that it was God who had spoken to them and told them to sit there until He came back. They sat where they were told to sit.

Soon God returned. He saw that they were obediently sitting where he had told them to. Next he said, "You girls are now to stand up and follow me. I am going to lead you," They walked.

Soon they came to a river that was running down to the earth. There was a raft there. They were instructed then to get aboard. "You girls get on this raft, but do not look down to the right side. You might get dizzy and fall off and die!"

The raft floated down the river, and suddenly it stopped. They didn't know that it was the Creator who was waiting for them there. They were told, "Get in a row, now, and follow me."

They didn't know what was going to happen to them. They followed as they had been told to do.

Soon they came to a village where there were many people, white people. They couldn't understand the language that these people were using. A white person came up and asked if they could understand. They said no. The people led them to a canoe and then took them across the river back to the raft.

The sisters got back onto their raft and continued to float down the river. The Creator, who was standing where the raft had stopped, told them to get in line again and follow him. He led them to some more people. These people also spoke a language which the sisters could not understand. One came up to them and asked if they could understand. When they said no, again they were instructed to get in line, and they were walked back to the raft.

They got aboard again, and the current floated them swiftly down the river. Suddenly their raft stopped, and they were told to line up and to walk upland, away from the river. It was the Creator who talked to them. When they arrived upland there were many people. Again these people used a language that the sisters couldn't understand. These people were Indians, but they all spoke a different language. Indians have different languages. The sisters were ferried back to their raft.

Now they got on board again and were carried back to earth. The Creator met them there when the raft stopped. He again instructed them: "Line up and follow me. We shall walk toward the east." They were taken over mountains, and they walked and walked a long way. They followed the Creator. He is also called the Changer, dúkʷibəł, in our language. The Creator placed the sisters where they were to stand. They were faced to the south and to the north.

Now the Creator called to the eldest sister, "Come, you will follow me now." They walked and walked. Suddenly she stopped. He turned to the eldest sister and instructed her to stand right on a certain spot. He put his hand on this eldest sister, and she immediately became a mountain, a white mountain. There was a little smoke coming out through the top.

As soon as she became a mountain, the Creator turned around and went back to get the next sister, the middle one. When he came to her he said, "You are to follow me now." She followed him. The youngest sister stood there by herself. The middle sister followed the Creator. She stopped when he stopped her and saw this big mountain in front of her. *She didn't realize it was her sister!* The Creator put his hand on her head, and very slowly she became a mountain also. She rose slowly until she became a tall white mountain with a little smoke also coming from her top.

When the Creator considered this, he said, "Oh, this will be a good legend for future generations to tell about!"

He returned for the youngest sister. She thought to herself as she waited, "What is going to happen to me now?"

The Creator came to her and said, "You are to come with me now!"

The youngest sister thought, "What shall I do?"

She obediently followed, however, and stood where she was told by dúkʷibəł, the Changer, to stand. He placed his hand upon her, and she slowly became a mountain. Before she had completed her transformation she saw the two mountains before her. She didn't know that her sisters had been changed into these mountains. The youngest sister didn't become a mountain quickly. Very, very slowly she turned into a tall white mountain that had a little smoke coining from the top.

The Creator observed his work, and he declared: "You folks shall just be legends for people in coming generations forever. You shall be visible to everyone, You shall be known as the Sister Mountains for future generations. You shall be mountains forever! Three sisters forever and ever."

That is the end of that legend.

{When storytellers discuss these mountains, some identify them as Baker, Rainier and Hood; some say they are the twin sisters by Mt. Baker, and others say they don't know where they are.}

Steelhead

Told by Susie Sampson Peter at Swinomish in 1953

IN LEGEND TIME, steelhead was traveling upstream. She swam upstream and arrived there at this creek which was called dxʷʔ(h)úptəd in legend time.

There she fished and fished, and she rendered the fat from the fish, and she put the fat into her container. Now she dried and dried her salmon as she prepared for her journey downstream.

When the season of the Frogs came, Steelhead heard them; then she turned to her children and said, "My children, it is time for us to travel downstream and go home. We have lots of salmon dried now."

Steelhead loaded all of her provisions. She placed her containers of salmon oil on the outside of her canoe, and she began her journey downstream. They traveled homeward.

Somewhere out on the ocean she met an old woman traveling. There were three others in the old woman's canoe: King Salmon and Dolly Varden were in the bow, and River Bullhead was at the stern. The old noblewoman, who was sitting in the middle of the canoe, asked her younger sister, "Is that Steelhead who must be going home now? We shall ask her. Maneuver our canoe towards her, and we shall ask."

They did this; then they called, "You must be going home!"

Steelhead answered, "We *are* going home."

Those in the canoe shouted, "How is the river? Has it flooded yet?"

Right away Steelhead got angry. She got angry right away! She retorted, "The river *is* big now. It *is* big now!" She snorted as she thought to herself, "I should be questioned about the condition of the river? Who are you to question my judgment? I'm questioned by the likes of King Salmon, who shakes his head around as if it had been chopped off!"

King Salmon did not say anything. He thought, however, "Did I say anything wrong to this one with a dirty nose, that she should curse and insult me?"

The old noblewoman swung her canoe across the bow of Steelhead's boat, obstructing her passage. She helped herself to some fat from Steelhead's supply. Steelhead's boat was turned off course. The people in the canoe said, "We shall take the fat from that person!" They turned Steelhead's boat off course, and then Dolly Varden swam on.

They took Steelhead's food and threw it into deep water, mocking her: "Now let us hear you holler your insults. You won't have any fat! Only in certain seasons will you have any fat!"

Dolly Varden was told that she would get fat at certain times. River Bullhead was given some eggs to nibble on as they went towards home.

When King Salmon arrived home he told everyone that Steelhead had insulted him. King Salmon complained, "She said that I look like someone with his head chopped off. For that, we cornered her and took away her fat."

Steelhead really shouldn't have insulted those people in that canoe!

There now, that is the end of what Steelhead and King Salmon used to do when they used to travel upstream a long time ago.

That is the end.

It is a short legend.

Yellowhammer and His Wives

Told by Susie Sampson Peter at Swinomish in 1954

YELLOWHAMMER AND HIS wives lived there. His wives were bears. Grizzly was one.

One day, Grizzly said to Yellowhammer's other wife, "Let us go berry picking. The salmonberries are ripe now." Brown Bear, the other wife, took a container, and so did Grizzly; and then off they went. They walked.

They found a good patch of ripe salmonberries, and they began to pick. Grizzly picked the yellow and gold ripe salmonberries and put them into her mouth instead of her container. They were so sweet and juicy!

Now it was time to go home, and her container was still empty; Grizzly snatched at the half-ripe berries that she had left hanging on the bushes before. She pulled these off and tossed them into her container.

Brown Bear picked beautiful ripe berries and put them right into her container. She didn't eat them. They looked so pretty there in the basket.

Grizzly said to her rival: "The lice must be making you uncomfortable. I could part your fur and look for the lice and try to get rid of them." Brown Bear agreed that it would indeed be good if they searched each other for lice.

As Brown Bear parted the fur on Grizzly's body, she found lots of fat brown lice.

But when Grizzly in turn parted the fur on Brown Bear's neck, Brown Bear slowly began to realize what Grizzly was after. Grizzly's strong, sharp teeth were going deeper than a search for lice!

After they had finished examining each other for lice, the women walked back home.

When Brown Bear was alone with her husband, she whispered, "My dear, your wife did something strange to me as we were out together. She bit my neck deeply while she was searching my fur for lice. Now you'll know that if I should happen not to return home, it will be because I am dead. Just take good care of our children if this happens."

The next morning Grizzly again invited Brown Bear to go out berry picking. When their containers were full, Grizzly suggested that they examine each other for lice.

As Brown Bear parted Grizzly's fur, she found lots of ugly burrowing ticks. She just picked them out and threw them toward the rotten wood. That is why you will find them there yet.

Brown Bear again confided her suspicions to her husband when they arrived back home from berry picking. She said, "If I don't return, it will be because your wife Grizzly will have killed me."

Grizzly dished up berries for her husband to eat. They were mostly green ones, since she had enjoyed eating the ripe ones herself. Yellowhammer picked and sorted out the slightly ripe berries and ate the few that he found. He then ate the berries provided by Brown Bear: they were delicious and ripe, and he ate until he had finished all of them.

As they prepared to go berry picking for the fourth time, Brown Bear said to her husband: "When I go, this time I shall die. Take care of your children until they are grown. Take care of them."

Yellowhammer listened and spoke kindly to his wife.

When the sun went beyond the horizon and it was past the usual time of Brown Bear's return, Yellowhammer turned to his children, and he said: "She must be dead. Your mother must be dead. The sun has set and she has not returned."

Grizzly suddenly returned with a pack on her back. She looked around as she spoke to her husband: "Didn't your wife get back? I hollered and hollered to let her know that I was starting back home, but she didn't answer me. I decided then that she had probably come on home before me. She hasn't arrived yet? Why did she walk so far away? When morning comes, I shall go out and see if she went so far into unfamiliar territory that she couldn't find her way back. I shall go far in my search for her and holler to her as I go."

Brown Bear's youngest child knows that Grizzly has killed his mother. He had watched Grizzly roasting something over the fire and recognized his mother's breast. When he shared this knowledge with his family, his father said: "The dirty thing has killed your mother!"

After Grizzly left in the morning, Yellowhammer was busy making arrows. He made arrows of soft charcoal for his Grizzly sons, and he made arrows of real flint for two of his Brown Bear sons.

Yellowhammer carefully instructed his Brown Bear children to kill his sons by Grizzly. He told them that they would not be injured by the arrows shot by their Grizzly brothers, because those were just made of charcoal. The children fought then, and Grizzly's sons were killed.

Yellowhammer now called to his Brown Bear sons and prepared them for what he knew was about to take place. He gave them berries and told them that these were to be given to the bushes in payment for their help. "Give the berries to Crabapple, Gooseberry and Wild Rose." He gave them feathers to pay Fir Tree Fungus. Then he gave his sons a spear and flint to be given to their grandfather, whose house was of flint. He instructed his sons: "Give this spear to Crane when she extends her leg as a bridge to help you. You tell her that Grizzly killed your mother, so you killed Grizzly's children, and you are trying now to get to your grandfather's house." Yellowhammer said to his sons: "I shall be nearby packing your youngest brother, and I'll just tell Grizzly a lot of nonsense when she asks about her dead sons. Walk quickly now, because Grizzly will be very angry when she comes. You look the area over carefully for a clear place to run. Hold your younger brother's hand. Help him and don't let him get hurt."

The boys went on. They followed their father's instructions and offered gifts to the bushes as they went.

Now the bushes grabbed Grizzly when she tried to get by them as she ran after the Brown Bear children. She angrily shouted Grizzly obscenities at the thorny bushes that were grabbing her.

The boys hiked onward, until they reached the shore where Crane was. They hollered at him: "Come across for us, grandfather Crane! Come across for us! Grizzly killed our mother, and we are going to our grandfather Flint's house."

Crane immediately stretched his leg across. He made a bridge for the boys to cross. When they had crossed to the other side, they said to Crane:

"Take this gift, which we give to you. Take this spear. When Grizzly comes along, you will just tell that dirty thing a lot of nonsense."

Crane accepted the gift and hurried the boys away from the angry Grizzly.

Crane wrapped his knees as he waited for Grizzly to come. He planned to pretend that his knees were wrapped because he was in great pain from boils. He was going to tell her how much this hurt him. He used cedar bark to wrap his legs, and there he lay as the sun went down.

Grizzly came to her husband, Yellowhammer, and she screamed at him: "Why did your children die, Yellowhammer? They are lying all over, dead!"

Throwing his voice, Yellowhammer mimics: "What is the matter, Yellowhammer, with your children that they are lying all over, dead?"

Grizzly yells furiously: "Say something, Yellowhammer, or I'll bite through you! Where did my nephews go, Yellowhammer? Where did they go?"

When Yellowhammer remained silent, Grizzly angrily pounced upon him and his youngest child, but he managed to fly out of her reach. He flew way up high. Yellowhammer can be heard from way up there.

Grizzly ran searching for the Bear children. She found their scent and she ran.

Yellowhammer positioned himself for a good view. As he scanned the surroundings for a glimpse of his sons, he worried about the difficult area they had to get through.

Grizzly lumbered forward. When she came to something she couldn't climb over, she would pull herself up and roll over. She would walk along the top of a foot log, then roll when she had to. When the thorny bushes grabbed at her as they had been paid to do, she would thrash at them with her powerful arms and bite at them with her big teeth. In this way she managed to crush the vines and free herself to walk on, thinking bitterly as she went: "Why do the dirty things detain me, when here I am crying in my sorrow over my sons?"

She went on. Soon she came to Crane down by the water. She asked: "Did my nephews go by here, Crane?"

Crane answered: "They went by. I have such a sore leg. The pain is just now easing a little from this boil on my knee."

Grizzly growled: "Stretch your leg across, Crane, or I'll chew you!"

Crane implored: "Don't bump my sore leg! Don't do it, or I'll have to jerk it."

Crane stretched his legs. He was screaming in pain by the time his legs reached across to the other side of the water. Grizzly now came walking across on them. Suddenly she stepped on Crane's knee. Immediately Crane jerked and cried out in pain. "Shwaa, shwaa, shwaa, shwaa!" he cried. Grizzly rolled off of Crane's legs and drifted downstream. When she found shallow water, she waded, but the river was mostly too deep for wading. So she managed to get herself to a calm eddy; then she climbed out of the water and ran upland, shaking herself several times as she went.

Crane unwrapped the cedar from his legs, muttering: "My leg was stepped on where it was bandaged, even though I asked Grizzly not to step on it." He flew up high to a place where he could look out. He could see Grizzly, but the children were out of sight. Crane thought: "They must have reached the house of their grandfather by now, and that is why I can't see them."

Grizzly went on, struggling against the bushes that grabbed her, crushing them. She kept asking, "Did my nephews go this way?"

Voices would mimic her as they repeated, "Did my nephews go this way? Did they go this way?"

Grizzly screamed: "Speak up, or I'll kill you! I'll chew you up!"

"Speak or I'll chew you from end to end!" Here—and again, over there— voices mimicked Grizzly.

Bewildered, she ran in every direction hollering insanely. Finally, she managed to get down to the water. She came to the house of Flint. There is his house. She went and she asked Flint, "Are my nephews here, Flint?"

Flint answered, "They are here. What are you going to do with them? They are here inside." Flint was crying. He was crying because Brown Bear had been his daughter. She had been his child, and now she was dead. He was crying. "They are here," he told Grizzly, "and what are you going to do with them?" He had a blade there, which had been provided by his in-law. He had made a door of it. His door.

Grizzly said, "Open the door! I am coming in! I want to see them!"

He said: "You can't come in. My doorway is hard to close. You can't come in. It is broken; it doesn't work like other doors, it is different. But if you *must* come in, you will need to come in backwards. It should be your butt which comes in first when you push it against the doorway. That is the only way you can manage to come in."

Grizzly said: "Oh, all right."

He raised the door just high enough for her hips to squeeze through; then he went. Now Grizzly came backing through. Just as she had her body halfway in, the blade fell. She was cut in two. Her back feet scratched about. Her front feet are outside, her front half running about biting at everything. It went down toward the water. It hurled itself forward. When it reached the water's edge, Grizzly bear died: it was only her front half there. When Flint saw that her front half was dead, he removed the blade and carefully placed it behind him so that he wouldn't get cut. It was very sharp!

Then he turned to his grandchildren and said, "We shall tie the legs of the dirty thing, and we shall float her away." Together they pulled her rear end to the water, and they rolled it until it floated away. They scooped up her blood and threw it into the water. They could see her front half lying where it fell. They rolled it until it, too, floated away. They could see her rear end bobbing up and down as it floated far down the river.

Flint's grandchildren told him that it was now time for them to join their father and youngest brother. They were to go as soon as they heard their father's voice call. Their grandfather told them that they could remain with him, if their father didn't come. But suddenly the children heard the voice of their father calling from the distant mountains. Flint said, "I wish to speak with your father, so I shall go with you when you go to him."

When they came upon Yellowhammer, he was sitting down trying to comfort his littlest child. Flint took this grandchild from the arms of his father, and he cried as he held him. They all cried, thinking of Brown Bear. Yellowhammer turned and spoke to his father-in-law. He told him, "From now on we shall be in the trees. I shall place myself and your grandsons in the trees forever! I shall place my youngest son on my head. He will be the red color you see on my head, as he is the last child that I have packed."

Flint answered, "all right. You have planned well to take care of your children."

"The dirty thing is drifting. Her body drifts down the river in two pieces," Yellowhammer said; "But you will always be able to see me here, always!" That is why you will hear Yellowhammer as he talks in the trees. He told his father-in-law, Flint, that he would be there. He took his sons, and they placed themselves there in the mountains.

Flint wandered toward home, mourning his daughter. When he arrived, he scraped and scraped the blood of Grizzly Bear and put it into the river, so that it would not cause his home to stink. He had a feeling of satisfaction that he and his grandchildren had bested Grizzly Bear. They had killed her!

From his home way up in the mountains, Yellowhammer could be heard as he talked. He said to his children, "We shall build our home in preparation for the cold winter. It will be in that huge tree." They hollowed the tree, making an opening just big enough for Yellowhammer and his children to go through.

Yellowhammer said to his children, "I am going to visit your grandfather down by the water. I shall tell him that our home is finished and that we shall be here always." He went then and told Flint that he had finished building a good home for the children. He had carefully prepared limbs from the cedar tree for their bedding.

Flint wrapped some dried dog salmon into a small bundle and took this home to his grandchildren. They happily took and ate this food from their grandfather, Flint!

That is the end.

Sockeye Salmon in Baker River

Told by Susie Sampson Peter in Skagit
(Northern Lushootseed) in 1954

qidáqiʔ AND HIS relatives lived there. They lived there below Baker River. He and his four brothers lived there with their mother. They are Magpies.

In berry season they go out and hunt for all kinds of berries, and they bring them.

qidáqiʔ heard about the wife of sə́ltups. He heard all about her wonderful qualities. He thought, "What a lucky man to have such a woman! (He most certainly can't deserve such a wife.) I shall go and take her away from him."

He told his elders what he planned to do. His mother loudly voiced her disapproval, as she sharply told him: "That would be a very bad thing for you to do—to take someone who already has a husband. Why don't you take a single woman?"

He quickly came back with, "Oh, that doesn't matter!—anyway, I am going after her: I shall take her away from that man from Point Roberts, sə́ltups.*

sə́ltups is always wandering away from home. Every day he goes some place, leaving his wife home alone with her relatives. She busies herself at her work, as she make blankets and clothing. She makes moccasins and leggings. The leggings are made of skin, and they are just tied. She also makes a kind of shirt that is just brought together through loops.

---

* In the Moses-Columbia language of Interior Salish, sə́ltups is a marten.

qidáqiʔ is from sbálixʷ in the Upper Skagit territory. Now he is on a journey, traveling and camping along the way.

Two days after he left home, his brothers came home from their hunting. The eldest immediately asked their mother, "Where is your son qidáqiʔ. He is not here."

"Oh, I am very unhappy about what your older brother is doing. I haven't been able to eat or sleep! He is going after a woman who has a husband. He is going to take her and bring her here. And is she the only woman who knows how to work, that he should persist in going after her? He will take her tomorrow, he said."

qidáqiʔ camped and he camped. His younger brothers began to follow and track him. They could see where he had camped. The morning finally came when qidáqiʔ was near enough to go after her.

qidáqiʔ had wandered off as usual across the water, where he generally went (pursuing and thinking of other women).

His wife proceeded to tend to her usual grooming. She took along the things that she needed when she went down to the water for her bath. She took urine. She took the eggs that she had soaking. She used these things as shampoo when she washed her hair. She walked on down to the water, undressed and washed herself, as she generally did, privately. She removed her clothes, got into the water and bathed, shampooed her hair—mmmmmmmm.

qidáqiʔ ran from his hiding place and stepped on her clothes. She washed her hair. Her eyes sting, yet she continues to shampoo her head. Then she washes herself. She dives, dives and tosses her head, as she rinses her hair.

qidáqiʔ is still there, silently standing on her garments. She glanced downstream a little as she wrung out her long hair. She pinned it up; then she turned around and looked: there is a person on her clothes. She said to him, "Oh, what you have done to me is bad! Why is it that you are confining my clothes?"

qidáqiʔ replied, "It is not bad! You are the reason I have come here. I wish to take you home to my land."

She answered, "Oh, I am not a single person. I have a husband."

qidáqiʔ said, "I know it, yet I am coming for you. I shall take you! I will not release your clothing until you agree! If you do not agree, I will not free them until night comes. I will be sitting there!"

The woman pondered her predicament. She thought, "Am I to blame, when what this man does to me is bad? His eyes have seen my unclothed body as I stood, walked around, and bathed." Feeling in her heart that she had been compromised, she said, "All right, but it will take me a long time to finish up my work. I have a blanket on my loom, and I shall have to separate and arrange my husband's things."

qidáqiʔ patiently answered, "All right. I shall be right over there waiting for you to finish. I shall wait for you."

She began to prepare herself. She loosened her hair that she had pinned up; she put on her clothes; and then, even though her hair is still wet, she begins to separate and arrange her husband's things. Now she combed her hair and put on her face paint; she put on her leggings and her moccasins. She puts all of her toilet articles together, along with her comb. She put her things together in her bag; then she spoke to her elders.

She said, "The day has come when I shall leave you. You shall never see me again! What my husband sə́ltups has been doing is just too bad. He has been leaving me every day, never thinking that I might be hungry or without firewood. I am still like a single person, having a hard time over wood, while I do all of my other work. He can be free to go wherever he likes to go when I have left you folks."

Her folks said, "Oh, that would be a bad thing for you to do, daughter. You had better change your mind about doing that. We would have no one to take care of us."

Their daughter stubbornly replied, "No one can stop me from going. I shall go ahead and go. You folks take good care of yourselves after I have gone. When I'm gone, sə́ltups can just go ahead and go where he likes every day!"

She put her things into a bag and took them outside.

Her father spoke to his wife: "You had better go and see which way your daughter is going."

Sockeye. These people are Sockeye. This woman that qidáqiʔ is taking is a Sockeye.

The mother watches as her daughter goes. As she reaches the base of one of the trees, a young man stands up and takes the woman's bundle, and they walk off together. The young woman just carries a new undergarment of pounded cedar bark that she has been weaving. They walk—mmmmmmmmmm. After they had gone quite a distance, she tore off a piece of her undergarment and threw it. It lay there. They traveled on until night fell, and they camped.*

qidáqiʔ's brothers came. They tracked him. They walked on. He was one day ahead of them. Suddenly they spotted a piece of pounded cedar bark lying along the ground. They gathered it up quietly. They gathered up the piece of undergarment of their in-law (the woman their brother planned to take as his wife). They picked up every shred of the cedar; then they began to sing:†

> We are only looking for
> Our older brother qidáqiʔ
> ????????????
> ????????????
> ????????????
> (laughter)

Again they sang:

> We are only looking for
> Our older brother qidáqiʔ
> ?????????????
> ?????????????
> ?????????????
> (laughter)

As she walked, the woman again looked to see where she could leave a piece of her undergarment. She tore off a piece and left it. (As qidáqiʔ's brothers followed, they again spotted it and picked up all of the shreds. As they looked for some place to throw them, they spotted a cluster of

---

* The woman is trying to mark her trail so that she could find her way back if she needed to.

† The brothers sang to let their brother hear and know that they were not the husband following after to retrieve his wife

ironwood burned at the base. It was there that they threw the shreds from their sister-in-law's undergarment.)

They followed along after their brother, and they camped where he camped, but way up high in the spreading branches of huge cedar trees.

When morning came, again they walked. After they had gone a long way, they found a piece of shredded cedar bark. They picked up the pieces and they sang:

We are only looking for
Our older brother qidáqi?
????????????
????????????
????????????
(laughter)

The woman (kept to her plan to leave a trail of her pieces of the undergarment she had been making). She looked for large maples growing side by side, and she tore off another piece and threw it up high into the branches.

The brothers had been following and camping now for two nights. qidáqi? was still ahead of them. They continued to follow, and when morning of the third day arrived they had traveled a long way, and again they found shreds of cedar bark and they sang:

We are only looking for
Our brother qidáqi?
?????????????
?????????????
?????????????
(laughter)

The woman looked for (a good place to throw her pieces)—mmmmmmm. Where could she throw them? Suddenly she found four cedar trees, and she threw the shreds there. There the pieces were caught on the cedar branches just hanging down all unraveled the way they had hung from the maple trees. (qidaqi?'s brothers as usual spotted the shreds and gathered them all up.)

qidaqiʔ went on. He arrived home with his wife, Sockeye. His mother saw her, and now she was very happy!

qidáqiʔ said to her, "Mother, I shall take your daughter-in-law to the base of the falls. I shall hide her there so that no one will find her, just in case her husband searches for her." qidaqiʔ took his wife's bundle, and he brought her to the falls.

{Susie at this point takes us back to the brothers who are following and has them gather up all the pieces of new undergarment that the woman has been throwing along her way.} After they have gathered up every shred, again they sing:

> We just look for
> Our brother qidáqiʔ
> ?????????
> ?????????
> ?????????
> (laughter)

{Susie brings us back to the woman who has been hidden at Baker Falls.} She and her husband qidáqiʔ are there. As the brothers come closer, they sing:

> We just look for
> Our brother qidáqiʔ
> ?????????
> ?????????
> ?????????
> (laughter)

It was night when the brothers arrived home to their mother's house. As usual they asked her, "Where is your son?"

She answered. "Your brother is not here. He took that woman that he has to the base of the Falls of Baker River. He is going to keep her hidden there!"

The brothers happily said, "Oh, we will see her tomorrow. Now we will camp. We are all very hungry." Their mother cooked them some salmon. They ate; then they went to sleep. They were all unmarried.

When morning came, they eagerly went to find their brother, who was there walking below the mouth of Baker River. They asked, "Where is your wife?"

He answered, "She is there at the bottom of the Falls."

His brothers said, "We would like to see her."

qidáqiʔ called her out. The brothers gazed! Oh, this Sockeye is a beautiful blonde woman. She quickly returned behind the spray of the Falls. She wasn't cold there.

qidáqiʔ told his brothers what he had in mind. He told them, "Your sister-in-law is going to be here forever! She will go no place! She will not go upriver! The people will all gather here for Sockeye!" This is the way qidaqiʔ then revealed the name of his wife.

{Susie tells us that Sockeye thus will come there every year, because qidáqiʔ stole her from (the Fraser River area, from Point Roberts).}

The brothers of qidáqiʔ asked their mother, "What will happen to her? Where will she go?"

qidáqiʔ looked at his mother and he said, "She will be there forever, Mother! Coming generations will come and gather here to fish for Sockeye."*

The following elders were consulted for help in translating this story: Martin Sampson (deceased), Helen Ross, Ida and Ray Williams (deceased), Theresa and Joe Willup (deceased), Lizzie Sampson, and Lottie (deceased) and Walter Sam.

---

* For a time the dam on Baker River prevented the fulfillment of this promise, but now in 1983 a few Sockeye have managed to return.

Moose

Told by Susie Sampson Peter at Swinomish in 1953

IT SEEMS THAT Moose and his father lived there. Wolf and his son lived in the next house. {It was winter, and the ground was covered with deep snow, so that food was becoming scarce.} The Wolves were always watching their neighbors for a sign of weakness so they could kill them and eat them. Moose was talking to his father, reminding him to be careful. Moose had snowshoes all ready for the time when he might have to make an escape. He said, "Oh, Father, we might be killed by our neighbors at any time." They whispered to each other all the time about this, saying, "Take care of yourself. You, too, could be killed without warning."

Finally, the day came when the father awoke and knew he was too weak to put up any resistance. Then he called out to Moose, "Run! I'm too old and weak now. I'm hurt." Moose called out to him, but the Wolves had already overheard.

Wolf said to his father, "We will divide them between us. The old one will be yours; the young one will be mine."

But Moose was ready for them, always on the alert. Just as his father was attacked, he jumped over the attacker and landed on the roof of the house, holding tightly to his snowshoes. Then he kept on running. Wolf came after, howling. Then Moose called upon the weather to snow. He wanted it to snow just enough to slow Wolf down. He wanted to be able to use his snowshoes.

It snowed just enough to bury the feet of Wolf and slow him down. Moose renewed his mourning, knowing that his father was dead. He went on, getting farther and farther away.

Suddenly, he came upon an old man who was carving. He coughed as he worked—cough, cough, cough. This was Mole, and he was making a hunting canoe. Cough, cough, cough, cough.

Moose asked, "Grandfather, will you take me across in your canoe? Wolf has killed my father, and his son is chasing me."

Cough, cough, cough—"You just pay no attention to him; ignore him."

Moose thought, "What kind of relative can I call myself so the old man will notice me and help me? He must have grandchildren." So Moose said, "I'm your grandson. Would you take me across the water?"

{This had the desired effect, and Mole told Moose to hide under his canoe while a decoy was made to misdirect Wolf. The decoy consisted of a poling stick and snowshoes buried in the snow across the river. Mole would mention the curious mound to lead Wolf astray.}

Much later, Wolf arrived with his sides all wet. He came to Mole and asked, "Oh, Grandfather, did you see the game I am chasing?"

Cough, cough, cough; cough, cough, cough. "Maybe along that point is where your game is going."

So Wolf ran to the point, but found nothing and came back. "There is nothing there. Maybe it is some place else?"

Mole was coughing again—cough, cough, cough, cough. When he was able, Mole said, "Maybe it is nearby. Possibly along the area downstream."

Wolf ran again, around two points, but found nothing and came back. He thought, "My game must surely be there, maybe a bit further, but still in range." He came back to Mole, who was still coughing. "I didn't find anything."

"See there! You are probably close. Your game probably went down-stream." Cough, cough, cough, cough—Mole was coughing as though about to breathe his last.

Wolf ran downstream, reached a point of land, saw nothing and returned.

This time, Mole was short with him. "Can't you manage to sneak up on your prey? Aren't you able? Your game goes downstream."

Wolf hurried to the point, found nothing and came back: "I found nothing!"

Mole only coughed: cough, cough, cough. Mole was now exasperated and thought out loud, "What can a man do? I am not at all well, and yet I get bothered!" Mole wiped his eyes: then he noticed something on the other side of the river. He shaded his eyes and looked across intently. He said to Wolf, "What is that lying down there, hiding across the river, a little upstream?"

Wolf immediately swam across. Mole said to his "grandson," "When Wolf gets across, you will turn the hunting canoe over." Wolf was still swimming.

Old Man Mole quickly turned over his new hunting canoe, and Moose, who was soon to be his grandson-in-law, pulled it down to the water and got aboard. He paddled up behind Wolf and hit him on the back of the head. He hit Wolf again and again. He hit Wolf three times to kill him. Moose pushed the body, and Wolf floated face down. Continuing across the river, Moose dug up his snowshoes and took them back to where Mole was.

Moose was crying then for the death of his father. He and his father had gone hunting, planning to have a good time until all this misfortune came upon them. To comfort him Mole offered his four granddaughters as wives. The oldest one cooked the game, and the youngest was great to laugh. "My youngest granddaughter is great to laugh—the slightest thing will set her laughing."

Mole called his granddaughters. He told Moose, "They will go around the room four times before they sit down. They will be quite a distance away when you first hear them, far away at the slope."

Suddenly, Moose heard someone coming. They were dancing and singing:

qʷáʔqʷałkʷədi qʷáʔqʷałkʷədi
qʷáʔqʷałkʷədi qʷáʔqʷałkʷədi
qʷáʔqʷałkʷədi qʷáʔqʷałkʷədi

His wives were coming, singing:

qʷáʔqʷałkʷədi qʷáʔqʷałkʷədi
qʷáʔqʷałkʷədi qʷáʔqʷałkʷədi
qʷáʔqʷałkʷədi qʷáʔqʷałkʷədi
qʷáʔqʷałkʷədi qʷáʔqʷałkʷədi

They arrived, came inside and danced; mmmm. . . . They had only gone around the room once when Mole spoke to caution them, "Be careful here of your husband. You are getting dust in his face." As usual, the youngest laughed: "Ha, ha, ha, hu! Grandfather, you always tease us about not having a husband." Then they danced and sang:

qʷáʔqʷałkʷədi qʷáʔqʷałkʷədi
qʷáʔqʷałkʷədi qʷáʔqʷałkʷədi
qʷáʔqʷałkʷədi qʷáʔqʷałkʷədi
qʷáʔqʷałkʷədi qʷáʔqʷałkʷədi

When they had gone around the room four times, they sat down. They took off their packs. Only then did the youngest see a man lying down. She thought, "So, what Grandfather said was indeed the truth." She asked, "Where is this person from?"

They were all seated, and their Grandfather spoke to them. "It is said that his father was killed by the old Wolf. Because of this he killed the young Wolf, who is floating away. Only the Wolf father remains alive, chewing on the remains of the Moose father." Knowing this, the wives accepted him.

The next morning the new husband spoke to his wives: "Oh, it doesn't matter that your Grandfather is weak, we will move up into the mountains anyway." Mole had no bow or anything else but his adze. He used this to make tools and to make wood shavings, yet the adze was not enough to protect the family; so they moved into the mountains for safety. The wives packed up all their possessions.

They started off, and Moose called out, "You folks clear a trail with sure footing for your Grandfather: then no one will slip!" They went on until they got to the hardest climbing. Mole was able to go ahead there, though. The one coughing to the verge of death could manage it. He came up quickly; right away he emerged from the place that was as steep as a cliff.

Someone probably lived on the other side—"That No-Good, who will pursue us once he has finished eating the old Moose, your relative."

On the side of the mountain, Mole found the wood and stone he needed to make bows and arrows with tips, the things he used in the hunt when he was a young man. He told Moose, "Fix up this rock for arrowheads. My bow is broken now; my arrows, too—they are rotten now!" Moose did as he was told and used the weapons to hunt elk. His wives butchered, prepared and dried the meat. They were able to dry much meat. They kept busy.

Suddenly, one day, they heard someone howling, and they knew that the dirty thing was coming. Mole made a plan: "You folks put these four small rocks into the fire. You folks heat them in the fire. Then we will wrap them in tallow and offer them to Wolf. We will roll each of them down his throat while he has his mouth open. He will be right here." {Moose kept out of sight so that Wolf wouldn't get suspicious.}

The wives kept at their work. Wolf arrived at the camp, saying, "This is a hard place to find. I am following a friend whom you may know."

He was told, "So, you are following after, following behind. Rest, now. Sit over there. The granddaughters will feed you like four proper wives. Just open your mouth, and they will roll this food down your throat."

Wolf does not suspect anything. His mouth is open, face pointed up, and the first piece of food is dropped down his throat. "Now just gulp it down. Enjoy."

Wolf gulps it down, swallows it whole. First the eldest woman fed him, then each of them by age. When the youngest one fed him, Wolf just stood there. There he stood. Suddenly, he fell over. The rocks had boiled in his stomach, and the tallow melted. He died and fell over backward. With a crash he tumbled downhill head first.

Moose said to Mole, "Tomorrow we shall go down to your house with all this stored food. We will pack it early in the morning." Mole carried a heavy load on the way down, because he was strong now. He took the lead with vigor. He quickly came off the mountain, using the trail cleared by the granddaughters.

Everyone followed and came to the house and camped there. Mole looked over the canoe he had been carving before and thought it very well done. His carving was very good. He warned his granddaughters, "Don't you folks ever leave your husband. Stay nearby while getting provisions. Strangers might come around and kill him. If you are far away, you won't know it." Then the old man finished the canoe, singeing the outside to make it sleek in the water. As soon as it was done, he used it to hunt with his grandson-in-law. As soon as he finished the canoe, the story was ended.

Basket Ogress

Told by Martin J. Sampson in Swinomish-Skagit in 1977

IT WAS SUMMER time. A group of children came to Swinomish on a picnic. A young boy, kikáwič, was given the responsibility of taking them there. He was a hunchback. He was also an excellent canoeman with good, strong arms, and he understood and respected the waters where he traveled. It took him several hours to paddle from kikiʔalus to xʷiwúʔc at Swinomish.

It was night when they arrived. As they settled down to sleep, the children were not aware of any danger. They didn't know about the Basket Ogress.

She came and grabbed the children. She put them one by one into her huge clam basket. kikáwič kept from being at the bottom of the basket by wriggling up over the other children. He *had* to take care of them: he was responsible for them.

When Basket Ogress had put all of the children into her basket, she went home to her house. It was upland from where the houses are now at xʷiwúʔc the village in Swinomish. Basket Ogress hurried toward her big house. She was thinking about her supper. kikáwič thought to himself as he bounced about inside the huge clam baskets: *My only hope is to try to get out of here and run away without her knowing what I have done.* As she stooped to go under the trees, Hunchback would reach up and try to grab a branch. At first he could not get a grip on the large branches. Each time he did this, the huge basket would jerk a little, and Basket Ogress would mutter, "My pack must have caught on something!"

Finally little Hunchback managed to grab a branch, and he pulled himself out of the clam basket. Basket Ogress kept going. Little Hunchback ran as fast as he could back to his canoe. He jumped in and paddled as fast as he could back to Utsallady. He told the parents what had happened to all of the children.

Basket Ogress finally arrived home and immediately built her fire bigger and hotter. She sang and danced as she thought about the good supper she and her own children would enjoy as soon as the rocks were hot enough.

As the children watched these preparations, the oldest one had an idea: "When she goes between us and the fire, we could push her toward the flames!" Together, then, they pushed her! She fell onto the fire, and they took little sticks and kept pressing her down.

Basket Ogress pleaded, "Help me to stand up here, you children!" The children replied, "We *are* helping you, but you are too heavy for us." (They are, however, just pressing her onto the fire.) They pressed her down until she quit moving. She died.

The children found their way back to the village at xʷiwúʔc. They were there when the people from kikiʔálus came looking for them. Hunchback had brought all the parents.

Oh! When Hunchback first went and got on board his canoe, Basket Ogress spotted him. She took rocks and threw them at him. That is why those little mountains are there. That is why the area of LaConner looks the way it does. Hunchback kept dodging the rocks, and she kept missing him. McGlenn Island, hayqíd, was created from one of those rocks. Swinomish was also created that way.

That is the end of this story.

Coyote Dances with the Sea Shells

Told in English by Alice Williams at the
Upper Skagit Reservation, August 31, 1984

THIS COYOTE WAS walking around there by the lake and he saw these women, Sea Shells. They lived in the bottom of the lake.

Every once in a while the nice, pretty shells would come out of the water and they were women. They would dance on the shore of the lake. They would come out of the water and they would sing songs and they would dance, and dance, and dance.

Coyote saw them. Every time he would see these women, he would try to get close to them. These women didn't like him. As soon as he would try to get close to them, they would all run and dive into the water. They didn't like him.

Then he got mad and then, he did that several times, and he got mad. So, he asked his Poop, "How can I get close to those women," he told his Poop. Then his Poop talked to him, "Well, this is what you are going to do. You see them when they are dancing and you go up to them and you dance for a long distance. You listen to that song and you dance for a long distance and you dance as you move along."

And at the same time, those women got tired of him, so they said, "Well, we are getting tired of Coyote coming and bothering us. We are going to take him down under water this time. We are just going to let him come. Let him come and we are going to take him into the water this time." So, when they came, well, they just stayed there and let him come. So, they had their plan made out. So, they didn't run away when he came.

They just let him come. And when he got there, he was sooo in love with those women! He didn't know what he was doing after they grabbed him and then he was in their midst now. He thought, *Oh, he was going to get married to those ladies now*. They had him by the arm. One on each side and they were just dancing around.

He was so in love, he didn't even know that they had him in the water now. And they kept going deeper, and deeper, and deeper into the water. He didn't even know he was in the water and they kept asinging, and singing, and moving him until he was up to his neck here now in the water.

Then pretty soon he started to squirm. He started to squirm around and they said, "Don't squirm around, we are going to take you home where we live. We want you. We want to marry you. We want to marry you, Coyote. We want to marry you. We want to marry you. We like you. Come on with us to our home."

He says, "No, no, I don't want to go down there in the water. But they took him anyhow. He got drowned. They drown him. They took him way down deep and they drown him and they let him go after they knew he was dead. He came uuuup. And he was floating around on the lake there, after he was dead now. He floated around and he got on the sand and old Wolf came along and found him.

"Oh, gosh, Here's old Coyote. He must have been fooling around with those Shell ladies here." He stepped over him and stepped over him, four times and then Coyote woke up.

He said, "Oh, why did you bother me when I'm asleep." There he was waking up. He had been sleeping for a long time.

That is the end of this story.

Grizzly Bear and Rabbit

Told in English by Lucy Williams
at Concrete, Washington, in 1954

IT WAS IN the winter, and cold, real cold. Rabbit and Grizzly were gambling at a sləhal game. Grizzly said, "Let's gamble, Rabbit." They were by the lake when they found each other. Rabbit and Grizzly both had a lot of Indian helpers on each side.

Grizzly got that sləhal and gave it to the helpers, and he held one himself. As soon as he got it he sang, over and over:

"Make a noise when you step
Make a noise when you step
Make a noise when you step."

He was singing about how he made a noise like a drum on the earth because he was so heavy. All the singers were happy.

Rabbit guessed the sləhal, and so his side got it. Rabbit was singing now,

"It's cold in the night, and blue sky" (all about the blue sky)

His helpers were singing and Rabbit was singing. They were singing at night. Rabbit always sings at night under a blue sky. He dances around and under the trees when there is going to be a blue sky. That's why rabbits make a noise, "Pupupupupupu," when the sky is blue at night, and they dance around a little tree.

Rabbit was busy gambling. Grizzly guessed but never got the sləhal. Then he got mad at Rabbit because he always missed. Grizzly was sore at Rabbit, and Rabbit kind of knew that Grizzly was mad. Rabbit thought, "We're going to get rid of that Grizzly after a while. He's always mean in this world." Well, he looked at Grizzly, and they were rather even now.

Then Rabbit said, "Let's play on top of that ice in the lake. We're going to roll balls on top of that ice." Rabbit shit little balls and made them big. He was a powerful man. They got one big ball. The ball looked just like a rock.

He talked to Grizzly: "Let's play on top. We'll have a good time. Come on, let's go! I want to show you my ball." Grizzly didn't want to go. But he went just a little way. Rabbit said, "I'm going to roll that ball and go way back on that ice. The ice is strong—frozen way to the bottom." He just said that. Rabbit went back and rolled the ball on top of the ice to the other end of the lake. He followed it and rolled it to Grizzly. They {Rabbit's side} were rolling it around and chasing it.

Grizzly just watched and watched for a while. Rabbit called him: "Come on, don't be scared! You won't sink." But Grizzly was scared because he was so heavy. "Come on. What's the matter with you? You know how to play ball!" Rabbit rolled the ball again, and then rolled it to Grizzly Bear. "Come on, now," Rabbit said.

Grizzly went a little further out, and the ice made a little noise. Grizzly said, "I'm scared and don't want to go further out." He {the narrator says *she*, now thinking of Grizzly as a woman} went out a little more and heard the noise again and went back. Rabbit rolled the ball to the other end of the ice and followed it and rolled it back to Grizzly, and it stopped. Rabbit called, "Come on! Let's play!" Grizzly went a little further out and was scared. Rabbit just said, "Look at me! I'm heavy, too, and I run around on top of the ice!"

Rabbit rolled the ball the last time—way, way out—and caught it and rolled it out again. Rabbit told his friends, "When Grizzly falls in, don't you help her out. Let her sink. We want to best her now, or she'll just kill in the next world." They got after Grizzly.

"Why don't you go farther out, Grizzly, and have fun? Go out a little further and play and have a good time."

Grizzly said, "All right. I'll go a little further."

They rolled the ball to Grizzly. She wanted to show off now, and she chased it around and rolled it. She got out on that thin part of the ice, and it broke and she sank. She asked for help. All the people on Rabbit's side just pushed and pushed her down. She kept hollering for help, and they just said, "Oh, we try to help, but you're too heavy." They kept pushing her down.

The end.

Skunk

*Told in English by Lucy Williams
at Concrete, Washington, in 1954*

SKUNK HAD TWO wives. He loved one and slept with her. But the other wife slept facing the other way. The one he loved, she liked that. Skunk always slept hard. In the morning he always farted a little bit on the other wife, and the smell of that thing was awful. The other woman, the woman Skunk loved, was all right. She didn't smell it much. But Skunk's butt was next to the other woman.

In the daytime, Skunk went out to hunt. The two women talked about it, because he did that every night. The other woman was getting all yellow and thin and had big rings under her eyes because she smelled that too much. After Skunk was gone, they talked. The woman who was getting sick said, "Not very long and I'm going to die. My husband farts on me!"

Every morning Skunk slept hard and then woke up. The sṗuʔ would be coming out of his ass, and the sṗuʔ would dance around the fire with a little bow and arrow like a little human, like a little child. After Skunk went out, the wife told the other wife about the little thing, Skunk's sṗuʔ, that looks like a little human. They talked: "What if we capture that little thing in the morning?"

Before daylight, about three o'clock, the little thing, the sṗuʔ, came out of Skunk's ass. The women said they would capture skunk's sṗuʔ and walk away with it. The sṗuʔ came out four times. And they would get up—easy, easy—to it. The woman in the back (who slept with Skunk's back to her) said that she would run away with it. Skunk slept hard and wouldn't wake up while the little thing came out.

She got up—easy, easy, easy. sṗuʔ started dancing around the fire. One woman jumped out and grabbed it and wrapped it up in something. Still Skunk was asleep. The two women walked away. "Well, we'll have a good time. We have a baby now. We'll walk to the houses of people and have our husband's sṗuʔ."

They were gone a long ways, and Skunk moved around and woke up. No guts! No insides or stomach! Nothing inside! Like a hole from ass to throat! He said, "No womans with me. My wives are gone!" He was staggering around the house, because he had no guts now.

The women were far away, and they came to a house. They had a good thing to surprise the people. The woman that stole Skunk's sṗuʔ was the one who owned it now. At night they sang at this house and called Skunk's name when the little dancer with the bow and arrow danced around and sang,

"I'm Skunk's sṗuʔ! I'm Skunk's sṗuʔ!
I'm Skunk's sṗuʔ! I'm Skunk's sṗuʔ!"

The little boy was happy and went even faster. All the Indians pounded the sticks and went faster, and he liked that. They said, "We like that," and kept going faster and faster.

Skunk got up and tried to walk around. He just staggered, because he was empty from ass to throat. He said, "I think I'll put something in my butt." He went and dug ferns and plugged that hole. He was all right, and he walked around pretty good now. "I'll find my sṗuʔ somewhere, later. I'll find my sṗuʔ with the women in some house up there." He was walking. He didn't feel strong, but he got along. He thought, "I'll get that white tree moss and put it on my head and be an old woman." He was going after his sṗuʔ in that place.

It came night, and the little sṗuʔ was going to sing again. Skunk was pretty close now. The only time he could get the sṗuʔ was while it was dancing around. He came in, and when the sṗuʔ came around, Skunk just whispered, "Are you my sṗuʔ?" The little thing just stared and listened. The other people just looked at that sṗuʔ, that little power. The little sṗuʔ went around again, and skunk whispered, "You are my sṗuʔ."

Otter was there watching the sp̓uʔ. Otter had no mouth, just eyes. He couldn't talk.

The fourth time the little sp̓uʔ went around, they all got happy and touched by that power. They saw the old lady who was just touched by that power. The fourth time it danced around, Skunk turned around and said to the sp̓uʔ, "Oh, just go in me, quick!" The little thing got in his butt real quick. And then Skunk p̓uʔ (broke wind), and p̓uʔ real hard. All of the people, even his own wives, died.

Otter was swimming in the river and wanted to tell the other people, but he had no mouth. Down the river the people said, "Cut the mouth open." Before that, Otter just went, "Mmmmmmmmmmm," and he tried to talk. Then the Otter was talking, and he told them that some bad thing was coming.

He said, "Skunk is down there, and he killed all of the people. He is coming this way."

They said, "We'll be ready for it." They had a meeting. "How are we going to kill him? If he comes, everything in the world will be dead. He'll be bad, if he is like that." They would have to beat him and kill him.

They went to the house. Otter told them to close it and make a hole in the roof, the only entry. They heated big rocks in the house. They said, "You tell him to come in and sit down." Well, Skunk was coming. Someone saw him. The big rocks were hot now.

Skunk went around the house looking for a door. "Where is the door in this house?"

He was told, "The opening is on the roof of this house."

Skunk climbed to the roof, and the people were ready. They had picked a very strong man to hold him down on the rock. When Skunk came in, he told them that he had lots of good stories to tell them. As he came down, the people were sitting down there.

They told him to sit on the red-hot rock. Now all of the strong men held him down on the rock to burn his ass. They said, "Go ahead and tell your stories!" Skunk just hollered and couldn't stand it. The people repeated, "Just behave yourself and tell your story!" He couldn't stand it, and he hollered. The men pushed him down, and he died. He was dead now. The men said, "You're just a little thing now. In the next world coming, your sp̓uʔ will be little and won't kill the people anymore."

That is the end.

Four Short Stories

*Told by Walter Williams in Skagit at his Longhouse
at Deming, Washington, in 1982*

Coyote Was Creating Rivers

As Coyote traveled around creating rivers, he neared the Colville reservation at Nespelem.

Coyote thought it would be good to find a wife here in this area where he was so far from his own homeland. He approached the people of Colville and announced that he was seeking wives from among them.

The shrewd Colville refused him!

In a rage, Coyote proclaimed: "You and future generations will pay for this rejection! I am not going to create a river that will go to your lands! You will not have any salmon!"

That's the end of the story. Now you know why there are no salmon upland at Nespelem. The Colville refused Coyote when he asked for wives from among them.

Skunk's Important Information

It was the season for the spirit dancing, and everyone was gathered there at one of the longhouses. They were gathered there. The people were there talking.

Someone came in. The people turned around and saw it was Skunk. He silently sat down.

The people spoke to him. They asked about his silence. "What is the matter with you, Skunk? Why don't you tell us your news?"

Skunk replied haughtily, "I have important news. I can't possibly take the chance of being overheard by someone listening outside the longhouse. I can't talk unless you plug up all of the cracks in this building so no one outside can hear."

One man spoke up and advised the crowd; he said they should go out and find some moss for all the cracks in the building. Soon they had all of the cracks stuffed with this moss.

The people all turned expectantly toward Skunk. What could Skunk's important information be? They turned around to face Skunk and listen to his story.

As they stood there waiting, Skunk turned away from them, raised his tail, and p̓uʔuʔ. Skunk killed all of them.

That is the end of the story.

Crane Saved Coyote's Life

Coyote was in agony! He had a bone lodged in his throat. As he coughed and gagged, he worried: "What shall I do now?"

Then his thoughts turned to Crane, and he managed to speak. "Crane has such a long neck, we should call him." Someone ran and found Crane.

When Crane arrived, Coyote gasped, "I seem to have a bone caught in my throat!"

Crane positioned himself by Coyote and began to work. He put his long neck down inside of Coyote's throat and found the fish bone and removed it.

This is why Coyote is alive. Crane did him a great favor by removing that bone.

That is the end of the story.

The Ticklish Bear

A man went walking out in the country. This person was walking. There he was walking. Then he came across a big bear.

Frightened, he thought, "Oh, what am I going to do now! I had better prepare for the worst!" He had heard many stories about how bear killed people. He was probably going to die!

The bear was practically upon him. It stood up. There he was!

The man tried to calm himself. "What shall I do?" He braced himself to accept his fate. Then—he knew what to do!

He walked forward. The bear was standing upright now. The man went forward and hugged the bear; then he tickled him. The bear lay down right away and went to sleep.

The man thought, "Goodness, I had better run now while the bear is asleep!" He ran quite a distance and then turned around to check on the bear.

There was the bear beckoning him to return!

That is the end of the story.

APPENDIX 1

Both the public and scholars are becoming more aware of the many facets of Native American literature. Now that it has become available in written form, many people are learning to appreciate its complexities. Recently, scholars like Dell Hymes and Dennis Tedlock have argued that these literatures are best treated as ethnopoetic verse, with measured rhythms and predictable phrasings. Some have called this contrived and over-complicated, but this technique does make sense of tiny particles (like gʷəl, huy, and ʔi) that otherwise seem unimportant. They clearly emerge as markers dividing up the narrative yet carrying the momentum along. Other important markers are the demonstratives where the middle -s- (as in tsi) specifies a female. As recast into a mythopoetic format, each word carries a full burden. As a sample of how this can work, we end with a favorite story. Since the next volume will be in Lushootseed and English, a taste of both is also provided.

s̓tatxʷ   ʔi   šišqačiʔəd
BOIL and   HAMMER

təlixʷ   suqʼʷaʔ
Fully-related   siblings (sisters)

   tiʔəʔ s̓tatxʷ   ʔi   tsiʔəʔ   šišqaqačiʔed
   this   Boil   and   this (ʕ: female)   Hammer.

haadᶻəlqid
long-haired

tsiʔəʔ   sťatxʷ,   ʔəsťəbš.
this (♀)   Boil,   braided.

gʷəl
And

tuʔuxʷ   tučəbəbiluɬ
(she) went out   to pick berries

bək̓ʷ   sləx̌il
every   day.

bək̓ʷ   sləx̌il
every   day.

tuʔux̌ʷ
went out

gʷəl
and

tučəbəbiluɬ
picked berries

tiʔəʔ   sali   təlixʷ   suq̓ʷaʔ,
these two   fully-related   siblings,

sťatxʷ   ʔi   šišqači?əd
Boil   and   Hammer.

bək̓ʷ   sləx̌il
Every   day

tuʔux̌ʷ   (h)əlgʷəʔ
Went out   they

gʷəl
and

tubəlkʷ.
returned.

x̌ʷuɬ sq̓ʷəlałed
Only berries

ti?ə? tus?ələds (h)əlgʷə?,
this was eatables (food) their

bək̓ʷ sləx̌il
every day.

t̓uk̓əxʷ
Going home now

?al ti?ə? dču? sləx̌il.
on this one day.

gʷəl
And

liłdᶻixʷ
went first

tsi?ə? šišqači?əd.
this (♀) Hammer.

gʷəl
And

liłłaq
came behind

tsiʔəʔ   st̕at̕xʷ
this (♀)   Boil

ʔəsčəbatxʷ
backpacking

tiʔəʔ sq̓ʷəlałed
these berries.

huy
And so

łčiləxʷ
arrived now

šišqači?əd
Hammer

dxʷʔal   ʔalʔal
toward   home

gʷəl
and

ʔaʔsil.
waited.

gʷəl
And

xʷi   gʷəsłčil
no   arrival

ʔə tsi   suq̓ʷaʔs
of this   younger sibling (sister).

huy
Well,

dxʷx̌ʷaq̓ʷigʷədəxʷ
she worried now.

bəlkʷəxʷ
Returning again now

dxʷʔal   ti   šəgʷɬ
toward   the   passage (trail).

ʔəydxʷəxʷ
Found now

ti?ə?   sq̓ədzu?
that   hair

ʔə tsi   suq̓ʷaʔs.
of that (♀)   sibling.

x̌ʷuɬ
Only just

sq̓ədzuʔs,

ʔa   ʔal   ti   šəgʷɬ.
there on   the   passage.

tiʔiɬ   x̌ʷəc   stab
That   sharp   whatever

c̓əlqayac
tree needle

tuɫʔal   ti   sčəbidac
from   the   fir tree

tuxʷiɫil   dᶻəɫ
fell down   must have

šəq(q)id
above the head

ʔə tsiʔəʔ   st̓aɫxʷ
of this (♀)   Boil.

gʷel
And

tuqʷəqʷ
busted (it)

x̌ʷuɫ
Only just

ʔuqʷəqʷ
busted!

x̌ʷuɫ
Only just

ʔuqʷəqʷ
busted!

xʷiʔ   gʷəšaw̓s,
No bones

x̌ʷuɫ
only just

sɬəbš
a braid.

ʔi,
Yeah,

x̌əɬəɬx̌əčəxʷ
felt sad now

tsiʔəʔ   šišqačiʔed
this (♀)   Hammer

gʷel
and

x̌aab
cried

gʷel
and

x̌aabicut
cried to herself

ʔal   tiʔiɬ   sʼtukʷs
upon that   reaching home.

gʷel
And

hədiw̓b
entered

ʔal   tiʔiɬ   ʔalʔals   (h)əlgʷəʔ
at   that   home   of theirs

gʷəl
and

ʔaʔəxʷ
was there now.

ʔi,
Yeah,

haʔlacutəxʷ
She stopped herself from crying now.

"ʔu.
Well,

łukʷiⱦ　　　　　čəd
will go waterward　I

　　dxʷʔal　ti　stuləkw
　　toward　the　river

čəda
and I

　　łučagʷusəb."
　　will wash my face.

huy
And so

　ƙʷitəxʷ
　went waterward now

　　dxʷʔal　ti　stuləkʷ
　　toward　the　river

gʷəl
and

ċakʷ
washed.

ʔəsǰadᶻ
Neck draped

    ʔə   ti   haʔɫ sqʷiqʷədqʷid
    with the   good necklace (♀).

qʷəcabšəd
Foot slipped

gʷəl
and

təǰ
rolled (she) {momentum took her}

    dxʷʔal   ti   stuləkʷ
    down into the   river.

yəx̌i
After all,

x̌ʷuɫ
only just

    tučəƛ̕aʔ
    a rock (she was inherently)

huy
so

ƛ̓əbaʔəxʷ
drowned now

    tsi   šišqačiʔəd.
    this (♀) Hammer.

diɬ shuys
That finishes (it).

APPENDIX 2

DATA ON THE TEXTS

CHARLEY ANDERSON, UPPER SKAGIT /sqaǰət/

Journey to the Sky and Back Down to the Earth

Loon with Deer Was Hunting Ducks with Bow and Arrow

The Basket Ogresses Chase Coyote

Wolf Brothers Kill Elk and Beaver

Boil and Hammer Are Living There

    Stories Told in English to Dr. Sally Snyder at Everson, Washington, 1954

    Slightly Revised by Vi Hilbert, 1983

LOUISE ANDERSON, UPPER SKAGIT–SALTWATER SAMISH /dxʷʔaha sʔabš/

Basket Ogress

    Told in Skagit to Dr. Pamela Amoss at Everson, Washington, 1962

    Transcribed and Translated by Vi Hilbert, 5 January 1983

EMMA CONRAD, SAUK-SUIATTLE /suiʔaƛ̓bixʷ/

Legend of the Seasons or All Year Round Story

    Told in Skagit to Dr. Thom Hess at Burlington, Washington, 28 March 1966

    Transcribed and Translated by Vi Hilbert, 7 February 1983

ANNIE DANIELS, DUWAMISH /duʔabš/

Fly

>Taped in Duwamish by Leon Metcalf (Reel 27) at Puyallup, 14 November 1952

>Transcribed by Vi Hilbert, 1980; Translated by Vi Hilbert, 22 November 1982;

>>Free Translation by Vi Hilbert and Dr. Jay Miller, 18 December 1983

AGNES JAMES, SNOHOMISH /sduhubš/

Basket Ogress

>Taped in Snohomish by Leon Metcalf (Reel 25) at Tulalip, 2 November 1952

>Transcribed and Translated by Vi Hilbert, 3 May 1981; Free Translation,

>>4 January 1983

ANDREW (SPAN) JOE, SKAGIT + SAANICH

Coyote

>Told in English to Dr. Sally Snyder at Swinomish /swədəbš/, 1954

MARTHA LAMONT, SNOHOMISH-SKAGIT

Mink and the Changer

>Taped in Snohomish by Dr. Thom Hess at Tulalip, 28 August 1963

>Transcribed and Translated by Vi Hilbert, 9 October 1982

Pheasant, Raven, and the Hunters

>Taped in Snohomish by Dr. Thom Hess at Tulalip, 12 August 1964

>Transcribed and Translated by Vi Hilbert, October 1980

Coyote's Son Had Two Wives

>Taped in Snohomish by Dr. Thom Hess at Tulalip, 1963

>Also Taped in Snohomish by Leon Metcalf (Reel 38), 1953

>Transcribed and Translated by Vi Hilbert, 13 May 1981; Free Translation

>>13 September 1981

The Seal-Hunting Brothers

>Taped in Snohomish by Dr. Thom Hess at Tulalip, 28 August 1963

>Also Taped in 1966

Transcribed and Translated by Vi Hilbert, December 1975 and January 1983;
Free Translation, 2 February 1983

Coyote Marries His Own Daughter

Taped in Snohomish by Leon Metcalf (Reel 50) at Tulalip, 1953

Transcribed and Translated by Vi Hilbert, 5 September 1981; Free Translation,
5 September 1983

Eyes of Coyote

Taped in Snohomish by Dr. Thom Hess at Tulalip, 28 August 1963

Also Taped, 22 June 1964

Transcribed and Translated by Vi Hilbert, 22 July 1974

Basket Ogress

Taped in Snohomish by Dr. Thom Hess, 2 February 1968

Transcribed and Translated by Vi Hilbert, August 1981; Free Translation,
3 January 1983

HARRY MOSES, SAUK-SUIATTLE (AND ENTIAT)

Legend of the Seasons

Told in English to Carl Cary at Marblemount, Washington, 1952

Revised by Vi Hilbert, 18 February 1983

RAY PAUL, SWINOMISH

The Legend of the Humpy Salmon

Taped in Swinomish by Vi Hilbert at Swinomish, 7 February 1981

Free Translation by Vi Hilbert, 7 January 1983

The Work of the Winds

Taped in Swinomish by Vi Hilbert at Swinomish, 7 February 1981

Free Translation by Vi Hilbert, 6 January 1983

The Legend of the Three Sisters

Taped in Swinomish by Vi Hilbert at Swinomish, 27 November 1981

Transcribed and Translated by Vi Hilbert, August 1982; Free Translation,
7 January 1983

SUSIE SAMPSON PETER, UPPER SKAGIT, SETTLED AT SWINOMISH

Steelhead

Taped in Skagit by Leon Metcalf (Reel 52) at Swinomish, 15 August 1953

Transcribed and Translated by Vi Hilbert, 14 October 1982

Yellowhammer and His Wives

Taped in Skagit by Leon Metcalf (Reel 56) at Swinomish, 16 March, 1954

Transcribed and Free Translation by Vi Hilbert, 6 November 1982

Sockeye Salmon in Baker River

Taped in Skagit by Leon Metcalf (Reel 24) at Swinomish, 2 November 1952

Transcribed and Translated by Vi Hilbert, 7 February 1978

Moose

Taped in Skagit by Leon Metcalf (Reel 42) at Swinomish, 19 April 1953

Transcribed and Translated by Vi Hilbert, 26 August 1978; Free Translation
by Vi Hilbert and Dr. Jay Miller, 12 August 1983

MARTIN SAMPSON, SWINOMISH-SKAGIT

Basket Ogress

Taped in Skagit by Vi Hilbert at Tacoma, Washington, 13 December 1977

Free Translation by Vi Hilbert, 3 January 1983

ALICE WILLIAMS, UPPER SKAGIT

Coyote Dances with the Sea Shells

Told in Lushootseed and English at Upper Skagit Reservation, 31 August 1984

Transcribed and Translated by Vi Hilbert, 1 September 1984

LUCY WILLIAMS, UPPER SKAGIT

Grizzly Bear and Rabbit

Skunk

Both Told in English to Dr. Sally Snyder at Concrete, Washington, 1954

WALT WILLIAMS, UPPER SKAGIT

Four Short Stories

Coyote Was Creating Rivers

Skunk's Important Information

Crane Saved Coyote's Life

The Ticklish Bear

All Told in Skagit to Vi Hilbert at Deming, Washington, 30 January 1982

Transcribed and Translated by Vi Hilbert, 29 July 1982

VI HILBERT, UPPER SKAGIT

sɫatxʷ ʔi šišqačiʔəd /Boil and Hammer/

Recast into Lushootseed, 9–10 August 1984

Rephrased into Stanzas by Dr. Jay Miller, 30 August 1984

SELECTED READINGS

FOLKLORE SOURCES

Ballard, Arthur. 1927. "Some Tales of the Southern Puget Sound Salish." *University of Washington Publications in Anthropology* 2(3):57–81.

———. 1929. "Mythology of Southern Puget Sound." *University of Washington Publications in Anthropology* 3(2):31–150.

Chapman, Abraham. 1975. *Literature of the American Indians: Views and Interpretations.* New York: New American Library. 357pp.

Clark, Ella. 1958. *Indian Legends of the Pacific Northwest.* Berkeley: University of California Press. 225pp.

Costello, James. 1974 [1895]. *The Siwash, Their Life Legends and Tales of Puget Sound and the Pacific Northwest.* Everett, Wash.: Paine Field Publishers. 195pp. (Dated and insulting.)

Culin, Stewart. 1907. *Games of the North American Indian.* Bureau of American Ethnology, Annual Report 24. Washington, D.C.: Government Printing Office. 846pp.

Egesdal, Steven. 1984. "Stylized Characters Speech in Thompson Salish Narrative." Ph.D. dissertation, University of Hawai<oki>i.

Elmendorf, William. 1961. "Skokomish and Other Coast Salish Tales." *Washington State University Research Studies* 29(1):1–37, (2):84–117, (3):119–50.

Haeberlin, Herman. 1924. "Mythology of Puget Sound." *Journal of American Folklore* 37(143–44):371–438.

Hedden, Mark. 1975. "Dispositions on the American Neolithic, an Introduction." *Alcheringa* 1(2):55–60.

Hilbert, Vi. 1979. *Yehaw.* Privately printed. 55pp.

———. 1980. *Huboo.* Privately printed. 153pp.

Hymes, Dell. 1981a. *"In Vain I Tried to Tell You": Essays in Native American Ethnopoetics.* Philadelphia: University of Pennsylvania Press. 402pp.

———. 1981b. "Particle, Pause, and Pattern in American Indian Narrative Verse." Working Papers of the 16th International Conference on Salish and Neighboring Languages. *University of Montana Occasional Papers in Linguistics* 2:202–49.

Jacobs, Melville. *The Content and Style of an Oral Literature: Clackamas Chinook Myths and Tales.* Chicago: University of Chicago Press. 285pp.

Kinkade, Dale. 1983. "Daughters of Fire": Narrative Verse Analysis of an Upper Chehalis
Folktale. *Papers in Anthropology* 24(2):267–78.

Kirk, G. S. 1970. *Myth: Its Meaning and Functions in Ancient and Other Cultures.* Cambridge
University Press.

Kroeber, Karl. 1981. *Traditional Indian Literatures: Texts and Interpretations.* Lincoln: University of Nebraska Press. 162pp.

Langen, T. C. S. 1984. "Four Upper Skagit Versions of 'Starchild.'" Paper of the 19th Conference on Salish and Neighboring Languages, Victoria.

Levi-Strauss, Claude. 1981. *The Naked Man.* Introduction to the Science of Mythology, Volume 4. Translated by John and Doreen Weightman. New York: Harper and Row. 746pp.

Matson, Emerson. 1968. *Longhouse Legends.* Camden, N.J.: Thomas Nelson and Sons.
128pp.

Palmer, Katherine Van Winkle. 1925. *Honne, the Spirit of the Chehalis.* Geneva, N.Y.: Press
of W. F. Humphrey. 204pp.

Roberts, Helen, and Herman Haeberlin. 1918. "Some Songs of the Puget Sound Salish."
Journal of American Folklore 31(122):496–520.

Sampson, Martin. 1938. *The Swinomish Totem Pole, Tribal Legends.* Told to Rosalie Whitney.
Bellingham, Wash.: Union Printing Co. 8opp.

Shelton, William. 1932. *The Story of the [Everett] Story Pole.* Everett, Wash.: Kane and
Harcus. 8opp.

Tedlock, Dennis. 1972. *Finding the Center: Narrative Poetry of the Zuni Indians.* New York:
Dial Press. 300pp.

Thompson, Stith. 1953. "The Star Husband Tale." *Studia Septentrionalia* 4:93–163.
Reprinted 1965 in *The Study of Folklore,* edited by Alan Dundes. Englewood Cliffs, N.J.:
Prentice-Hall.

Wickersham, James. 1898. "Nisqually Mythology." *Overland Monthly,* Series 2, 32.

HISTORICAL SOURCES

Bagley, Clarence. 1980 [1905]. *In the Beginning: Early Days on Puget Sound.* Everett, Wash.:
Historical Society of Seattle and King County. 88pp.

Denny, Emily Inez. 1909. *Blazing the Way: True Stories, Songs and Sketches of Puget Sound
and Other Pioneers.* Seattle: Rainier Printing Co. 504pp.

Duwamish Tribe and others. 1933. Consolidated Petition in the United States Court of
Claims. 2 Volumes.

Eels, Reverend Myron. 1884. "Census of the Clallam and Twana Indians of Washington
Territory." *American Antiquarian* 6:35–38.

———. 1887. "The Indians of Puget Sound" (in nine parts). *American Antiquarian* 9.

———. 1889. "The Twana, Chemakum, and Klallam Indians of Washington Territory."
Smithsonian Annual Report for 1887:605–81.

Gibbs, George. 1876. *Tribes of Western Washington and Northwestern Oregon.* Part 2,
pp. 157–241. Washington, D.C.: Department of the Interior, United States Geographical
and Geological Survey of the Rocky Mountain Region.

———. 1970. "Dictionary of the Niskwalli (Nisqually) Indian Language—Western Washington." Extract from the 1877 *Contributions to North American Ethnology* 1:285–361. Seattle: Shorey Book Store Facsimile Reproductions.

Horr, David Agee. 1974. *Coast Salish and Western Washington Indians v. Indian Claims Commission. Findings.* New York: Garland Publishing. 66opp.

Meany, Edmund. 1957 [1907]. *Vancouver's Discovery of Puget Sound: Portraits and Biographies of the Men Honored in the Naming of the Geographical Features of Northwestern America.* Portland: Binford and Mort. 40opp.

Sampson, Martin. 1972. *Indians of Skagit County.* Mount Vernon, Wash.: Skagit County Historical Society, Series 2.

Watt, Roberta Frye. 1931. *Four Wagons West: The Story of Seattle.* Portland: Binford and Mort. 39opp.

White, Richard. 1980. *Land Use, Environment, and Social Change: The Shaping of Island County, Washington.* Seattle: University of Washington Press. 234pp.

Wilkes, Charles. 1849. *Narrative of the United States Exploring Expedition.* Philadelphia: n.p.

ETHNOGRAPHIC SOURCES

Abbott, Donald. 1981. *The World Is as Sharp as a Knife: An Anthology in Honour of Wilson Duff.* Victoria: British Columbia Provincial Museum. 343pp.

Amoss, Pamela. 1975. "Catalogue of the Marian Smith Collection of Fieldnotes, Manuscripts, and Photographs." Manuscript. Library of the Royal Anthropological Institute of Great Britain and Ireland, London. 25pp.

———. 1978. *Coast Salish Spirit Dancing: The Survival of an Ancestral Religion.* Seattle: University of Washington Press. 193pp.

Ballard, Arthur. 1950. "Calendric Terms of the Southern Puget Sound Salish." *Southwestern Journal of Anthropology* 6(1):79–99.

———. 1957. "The Salmon Weir on the Green River in Western Washington." *Davidson Journal of Anthropology* 3:37–55.

Barnett, Homer. 1955. *The Coast Salish of British Columbia.* Studies in Anthropology 4. Eugene: University of Oregon Press. 320pp.

———. 1957. *Indian Shakers: A Messianic Cult of the Pacific Northwest.* Carbondale: Southern Illinois University Press. 378pp.

Carlson, Barry, and Thom Hess. 1978. "Canoe Names in the Northwest, an Areal Study." *Northwest Anthropological Research Notes (NARN)* 12:17–24.

Collins, June. 1950. "Growth of Class Distinctions and Political Authority Among the Skagit Indians during the Contact Period." *American Anthropologist* 52(3):331–42.

———. 1952. "The Mythological Basis for Attitudes toward Animals among the Salish-Speaking Indians." *Journal of American Folklore* 65(258):353–59.

———. 1966. "Naming, Continuity, and Social Inheritance among the Coast Salish of Western Washington." *Papers of the Michigan Academy of Science, Arts, and Letters* 51:425–36.

———. 1974. *Valley of the Spirits: The Upper Skagit Indians of Western Washington*. Seattle: University of Washington Press. 267pp.

Curtis, Edward. 1913. *The North American Indian*. Volume 9, *Salishan Tribes of the Coast, the Chimakum and the Quilliute, the Willapa*. Norwood, Mass.: Plimpton Press.

Densmore, Frances. 1943. *Music of the Indians of British Columbia*. Bureau of American Ethnology, Bulletin 136, Anthropological Paper 27. Washington, D.C.: Government Printing Office. 109pp.

Dorsey, George. 1902. "The Duwamish Spirit-Canoe and Its Use." *Bulletin of the Free Museum of Science and Art, University of Pennsylvania* 3(4):227–38.

Elmendorf, William. 1946. "Twana Kinship Terminology." *Southwestern Journal of Anthropology* 2:420–32.

———. 1948. "The Cultural Setting of the Twana Secret Society." *American Anthropologist* 50:625–633.

———. 1961. "System Change in Salish Kinship Terminologies." *Southwestern Journal of Anthropology* 17(4):365–82.

———. 1970. "Skokomish Sorcery, Ethics, and Society." In *Systems of North American Witchcraft and Sorcery*, edited by Deward Walker, 147–82. Anthropological Monographs of the University of Idaho 1. Moscow: University of Idaho. 295pp.

———. 1971. "Coast Salish Status Ranking and Intergroup Ties." *Southwestern Journal of Anthropology* 27:353–81.

Elmendorf, William, and Alfred Kroeber. 1960. *The Structure of Twana Culture*. Pullman: Washington State University Research Studies, Monographic Supplement 2. 576pp.

Gunther, Erna. 1974. *Ethnobotany of Western Washington: The Knowledge and Use of Indigenous Plants by Native Americans*. Seattle: University of Washington Press. 71pp.

Harrington, John P. 1910. Fieldnotes from Lummi and Duwamish. Microfilm available at Northwest Special Collection, Suzzallo Library, University of Washington.

———. 1942. Fieldnotes from Chemakum, Clallam, Makah, and Quileute. Microfilm available at Northwest Special Collection, Suzzallo Library, University of Washington.

Haeberlin, Herman. 1918. "SbEtEda'q, a Shamanic Performance of the Coast Salish." *American Anthropologist* 20(3):249–257.

Haeberlin, Herman, and Erna Gunther. 1930. "The Indians of Puget Sound." *University of Washington Publications in Anthropology* 4(1):1–84.

Hess, Thom, and Vi Hilbert. 1977. "Recording in the Native Language." *Sound Heritage* 4:4–32.

Hilbert, Vi. 1980. *Ways of the Lushootseed People: Ceremonies and Traditions of the Northern Puget Sound Indians*. Seattle: United Indians of All Tribes Foundation, Daybreak Star Press. 56pp.

Howay, F. W. 1918. "The Dog's Hair Blankets of the Coast Salish." *Washington Historical Quarterly* 9(2):83–92.

Hulse, Frederick. 1957. "Linguistic Barriers to Gene-Flow; the Blood-Groups of the Yakima, Okanogan, and Swinomish Indians." *American Journal of Physical Anthropology* 15(2):235–46.

Jelik, Wolfgang. 1982. *Indian Healing: Shamanic Ceremonialism in the Pacific Northwest Today.* Surrey, British Columbia:. Hancock House Publishers. 182pp.

Knight, Rolf. 1978. *Indians at Work: An Informal History of Native Indian Labour in British Columbia, 1858–1930.* Vancouver: New Star Books. 320pp.

Singh, Ram Raj Prasad. 1966. *Aboriginal Economic System of the Olympic Peninsula Indians.* Sacramento Anthropological Society Paper 4. Sacramento: Sacramento State College. 140pp.

Smith, Marian. 1940. *The Puyallup-Nisqually.* Columbia University Contributions to Anthropology 32. New York: Columbia University Press. 336pp.

———. 1941. "The Coast Salish of Puget Sound." *American Anthropologist* 43:197–211.

———, ed. 1949. *Indians of the Urban Northwest.* Columbia University Contributions to Anthropology 36. New York: Columbia University Press. 370pp.

Snyder, Sally. 1964. "Skagit Society and Its Existential Basis: An Ethnofolkloristic Reconstruction." Ph.D. dissertation, University of Washington. 495pp.

———. 1975. "Quest for the Sacred in Northern Puget Sound: An Interpretation of the Potlatch." *Ethnology* 14(2):149–61.

Spier, Leslie. 1936. *Tribal Distribution in Washington.* General Series in Anthropology 1. Menasha, Wisc.: George Banta Publishing Company. 43pp.

Stewart, Hilary. 1982. *Indian Fishing: Early Methods on the Northwest Coast.* Seattle: University of Washington Press. 181pp.

Suttles, Wayne. 1951. "Economic Life of the Coast Salish of Haro and Rosario Straits." Ph.D. dissertation, University of Washington. 513pp.

———. 1952. "Notes on Coast Salish Sea-Mammal Hunting." *Anthropology in British Columbia* 3:10–20.

———. 1954. "Post-contact Culture Change among the Lummi Indians." *British Columbia Historical Quarterly* 18(1–2):29–102.

———. 1957. "The Plateau Prophet Dance among the Coast Salish." *Southwestern Journal of Anthropology* 13(4):352–96.

———. 1958. "Private Knowledge, Morality, and Social Classes among the Coast Salish." *American Anthropologist* 60:497–507.

———. 1960. "Affinal Ties, Subsistence, and Prestige among the Coast Salish." *American Anthropologist* 62(2):295–305.

———. 1962. "Variation in Habitat and Culture on the Northwest Coast." In *Akten des 34. Internationalen Amerikanistenkongresses, Wien, 1960,* 522–37. Vienna: Verlag Ferdinand Berger.

———. 1963. "The Persistence of Intervillage Ties among the Coast Salish." *Ethnology* 2(4):512–25.

———. 1968. "Coping with Abundance: Subsistence on the Northwest Coast." In *Man the Hunter,* edited by Richard Lee and Irven DeVore, 55–68. Chicago: Aldine.

———. 1972. "On the Cultural Track of the Sasquatch." *Northwest Anthropological Research Notes* 6(1):65–90.

———. 1977. "The 'Coast Salish' of the Georgia-Puget Sound—Another Look." *Puget Soundings* (April):22–25.

————. 1980. "Sasquatch: The Testimony of Tradition." In *Manlike Monsters on Trial*, edited by Marjorie Halpin and Michael Ames, 245–54. Vancouver: University of British Columbia Press.

Turner, Nancy. 1975. *Food Plants of British Columbia Indians*. Part 1, *Coastal Peoples*. Victoria: British Columbia Provincial Museum, Handbook 34. 265pp.

Waterman, Thomas T., and Geraldine Coffin. 1920. *Types of Canoes on Puget Sound*. Indian Notes and Monographs. New York: Museum of the American Indian, Heye Foundation. 43pp.

————. 1922. "The Geographical Names Used by the Indians of the Pacific Coast." *Geographical Review* 12(2):175–94.

————. 1930. "The Paraphernalia of the Duwamish 'Spirit-Canoe' Ceremony." *Indian Notes* 7(2):129–48, 295–312, 535–61.

————. 1973. *Notes on the Ethnology of the Indians of Puget Sound*. Indian Notes and Monographs, Miscellaneous Series 59. New York: Museum of the American Indian, Heye Foundation. 96pp. and 45 plates.

Waterman, Thomas T., Geraldine Coffin, and others. 1921. *Native Houses of Western North America*. Indian Notes and Monographs. New York: Museum of the American Indian, Heye Foundation. 97pp.

Wike, Joyce. 1952. "The Role of the Dead in Northwest Coast Culture." In *Indian Tribes of Aboriginal America*, proceedings of the 29th International Congress of Americanists 3, edited by Sol Tax, 97–103. Chicago: University of Chicago Press.

LINGUISTIC SOURCES

Boas, Franz, and Herman Haeberlin.1927. "Sound Shifts in Salishan Dialects." *International Journal of American Linguistics* 4:117–36.

Drachman, Gaberell. 1969. *Twana Phonology*. Working Papers in Linguistics 5. Columbus: Ohio State University. 286pp.

Efrat, Barbara, ed. 1979. *The Victoria Conference on Northwestern Languages: Victoria, British Columbia, November 4–5, 1976*. Heritage Record 4. Victoria: British Columbia Provincial Museum. 176pp.

Galin, Anne. 1982. "The Encoding of Spatial Relations in Lushootseed." Paper of the 17th Conference on Salish and Neighboring Languages, Portland.

————. 1983. "Spatial Organization of Lushootseed Culture, Texts, and Language." Ph.D. dissertation, Columbia University.

————. 1984. "Cognitive Configuration in Lushootseed." Paper of the 19th Conference on Salish and Neighboring Languages, Victoria.

Haeberlin, Herman. 1974. "Distribution of the Salish Substantive [Lexical] Suffixes." Edited by M. Terry Thompson. *Anthropological Linguistics* 16(6):219–350.

Hess, Thom. 1966. "Snohomish Chameleon Morphology." *International Journal of American Linguistics* 32:350–56.

————. 1967. "The Morph –əb in Snohomish." Paper of the 2nd International Conference on Salish Languages, Seattle.

———. 1968. "Directive Phrases: A Consideration of One Facet of Puget Salish Syntax." Paper of the 3rd International Conference on Salish Languages, Victoria.

———. 1969. "Secondary Suffixation in Puget Salish." Paper of the 4th International Conference on Salish Languages, Victoria.

———. 1971. *Prefix Constituents with /x^w/.* Studies in Northwest Indian Languages. Sacramento Anthropological Society Paper 11. Sacramento: Sacramento State College.

———. 1972. "Some Lexical Sets in Puget Salish Orientation Vocabulary." Paper of the 7th International Conference on Salish Languages, Bellingham.

———. 1973a. "Agent in a Coast Salish Language." *International Journal of American Linguistics* 39:89–94.

———. 1973b. "On Pedagogical Grammar for Salish Languages." Paper of the 8th International Conference on Salish Languages, Eugene.

———. 1974. "How Do You Say 'You Are My Father' in Salish?" Paper of the 9th International Conference on Salish Languages, Vancouver.

———. 1975a. "A Note on ʔə Constructions in Lushootseed." Paper of the 10th International Conference on Salish Languages, Ellensburg.

———. 1975b. "Planning a Language Programme." In *Write On: A Sourcebook for Teachers of Indian Languages and Writing Systems*, edited by J. Wild and J. Rathjen, 43–46. Williams Lake, B.C.: Fish Lake Cultural Education Centre.

———. 1976a. *Dictionary of Puget Salish.* Seattle: University of Washington Press. 771pp.

———. 1976b. "Lushootseed Dialects and the Saanich Lexicon." Paper of the 3rd Annual Meeting of the Canadian Ethnology Society, Victoria.

———. 1977. "Lushootseed Dialects." *Anthropological Linguistics* 19(9):403–19.

———. 1979a. "A Comparison of Marine and Riverine Orientation Vocabulary in Two Coast Salish Languages." *Anthropological Linguistics* 21(8):363–78.

———. 1979b. "Central Coast Salish Words for Deer: Their Wavelike Distribution. *International Journal of American Linguistics* 45:5–16.

———. 1980. "Dictionary of Puget Salish." Paper of the Conference on Lexicography in the New World Context, Albuquerque.

———. 1982. "Traces of 'Abnormal' Speech in Lushootseed." Paper of the 17th International Conference on Salish and Neighboring Languages, Portland.

———. 1984. "Morphological Spelling for Pedagogical and Other Practical Purposes." Paper of the 19th International Conference on Salish and Neighboring Languages, Victoria.

Hess, Thom, and Vi Hilbert. 1975a. *Lushootseed: The Language of the Skagit, Nisqually, and Other Tribes of Puget Sound; An Introduction.* Books 1 and 2. Seattle: Daybreak Star Press. 195pp.

———. 1975b. "Recording in the Native Language." *Sound Heritage* 4(3):38–42.

———. 1977. *Lushootseed.* Book 2. Seattle: Daybreak Star Press. 225pp.

———. 1982. "The Lushootseed Language Project." In *Language Renewal among American Indian Tribes: Issues, Problems, and Prospects*, edited by Robert St. Clair and William Leap, chapter 6. Roselyn, Va.: National Clearinghouse for Bilingual Education.

Hilbert, Vi. 1974. "On Transcribing the Metcalf Tapes." Paper of the 9th International Conference on Salish Languages, Vancouver.

———. 1976. "Fieldwork Report." Paper of the 11th International Conference on Salish and Neighboring Languages, Seattle.

———. 1983. "Poking Fun in Lushootseed." Paper of the 18th International Conference on Salish and Neighboring Languages, Seattle.

Hilbert, Violet, and Thom Hess. 1978. "Lushootseed: How Daylight Was Stolen." *International Journal of American Linguistics, Native American Texts Series* 2:4–32.

Jacobs, Melville. 1937. "Historical Perspectives in Indian Languages of Oregon and Washington." *Pacific Northwest Quarterly* 28:55–74.

Jorgensen, Joseph. 1969. *Salish Language and Culture: A Statistical Analysis of Internal Relationships, History, and Evolution.* Language Science Monographs 3. Bloomington: Indiana University. 173pp.

Kinkade, Dale. 1983. "Salish Evidence against the Universality of 'Noun' and 'Verb.'" *Lingua* 60:25–40.

Pilling, James. 1893. *Bibliography of the Salishan Languages.* Bureau of American Ethnology, Bulletin 16. Washington, D.C.: Government Printing Office. 100pp.

Ransom, Jay Ellis. 1945. "Notes on Duwamish Phonology and Morphology." *International Journal of American Linguistics* 11(4):204–10.

Snyder, Warren. 1968a. *Southern Puget Sound Salish: Phonology and Morphology.* Sacramento Anthropological Society Paper 8. Sacramento: Sacramento State College. 83pp.

———. 1968b. *Southern Puget Sound Salish: Texts, Place Names, and Dictionary.* Sacramento Anthropological Society Paper 9. Sacramento: Sacramento State College. 199pp.

Suttles, Wayne, and William Elmendorf. 1960. "Pattern and Change in Halkomelem Salish Dialects." *Anthropological Linguistics* 2:1–32.

———. 1963. "Linguistic Evidence for Salish Prehistory." In *Symposium on Language and Culture*, proceedings of the 1962 Annual Spring Meeting of the American Ethnological Society, edited by Viola Garfield and Wallace Chafe, 41–52. Seattle: University of Washington Press.

Thompson, Laurence. 1973. "The Northwest." *Current Trends in Linguistics*, Volume 10, *Linguistics in North America*, edited by Thomas Sebeok, 979–1045. The Hague: Mouton.

———. 1979. "Salishan and the Northwest." *The Languages of Native America*, edited by Lyle Campbell and Marianne Mithun, 692–765. Austin: University of Texas Press.

Twedell, Colin. 1950. "The Snoqualmie-Duwamish Dialects of Puget Sound Salish." *University of Washington Publications in Anthropology* 12:1–78.